Live, Learn, Love:

Rediscover Your Life Purpose in 10 Days

Live, Learn, Love:
Rediscover Your Life Purpose in 10 Days

Gale Minchew, PhD and Karen Lovero

Live, Learn, Love: Rediscovering Your Life Purpose in 10 Days

Cover image courtesy of Gerd Altmann via Pixabay.com
Cover design by Gale Minchew

Gale Minchew
For ordering and more information visit www.galeminchew.com/Books

First Edition: September 2015

Unless otherwise noted, the names used in this book have been changed to protect the individual's privacy.

Disclaimer: The material in this book is not intended to replace medical, mental health, or other professional services. Please continue or seek treatment as prescribed or recommended by your professional services providers.

ISBN-13: 978-0-9838301-5-3

Printed in the United States of America

This book is dedicated to our husbands and children. Your love and grace have helped us immensely in the creation of this work. Our love is yours eternally...

Table of Contents

Introduction   ix

Chapter 1: I Am the Light   1

    Life Purpose Prayer Part I   2

Chapter 2: My Mission Is Guided By Truth   13

    Life Purpose Prayer Part II   14

    Meditation: Recognizing and Interpreting

    Signs From Above   18

Chapter 3: I Live In Balance and Harmony   23

    Spiritual Request: Balance and Harmony   28

    Mental Exercise   29

    Wisdom Prayer   33

Chapter 4: I Am Change   37

    Signs of Guidance Prayer   38

    Mental Exercise   42

    Spiritual Request: Welcoming Change   45

Chapter 5: I Release All That No Longer Serves Me   49

    Mental Exercise   51

    Meditation: Cutting Cords with Archangel

    Michael   54

Chapter 6: I Reject Past Life Limitations   59

    Spiritual Request to Reinstate Spiritual Gifts   63

    Spiritual Request to Release Past Life Vows   68

    Soul Contract Prayer   71

Chapter 7: I Reject Fear   75

    Meditation: Releasing Fear with Archangels

    Michael and Uriel   78

Chapter 8: I Release Unhealthy Spiritual Contracts   85

    Releasing Contracts Prayer   88

    Meditation: Soul Confessions with

    Archangel Michael   89

Chapter 9: I Trust My Divine Self   99

Chapter 10: I Forgive Myself and Others   119

    Spiritual Request for Self-Forgiveness   122

    Releasing Unforgiveness Prayer   124

    Meditation: Releasing the Weight of

    Unforgiveness   126

    Meditation: Rewriting the Past for Healing   129

    Meditation: Mending a Broken Heart   132

    Meditation: Forgiving the Past   135

    Letter Writing Technique   139

    Spoken Work Technique   141

Final Thoughts   145

About the Authors   149

Introduction

Less than a year ago, Spirit put us in contact with one another through social media. Despite the spiritual advancements Dr. Gale had made over time, she remained in the "spiritual closet" with one foot in her 3D reality as a psychologist and the other foot attempting to walk her spiritual path. At the same time, Karen was effectively out of the closet, conducting Angelic readings, sharing her channeling gifts, and living her truth.

From the beginning of our friendship in October 2014 to meeting in person for the first time in January 2015 and beginning this book in March 2015, our paths have been divinely guided. At the outset, we had no idea that we would be writing a book together. Somewhere along the way, in those few short months, the Angels guided, supported, and encouraged us to share our gifts with the world.

This project began with the foundations for the Life Purpose Prayer presented within this book. Karen channeled this prayer from the Angels along with several other messages and prayers intended to help us rediscover and truly live within our life purpose. She forwarded this material to Dr. Gale who began separating it into chapters, editing content, and adding meditations. Over a few short months these simple excerpts of information began to take shape into the guide book before you, filled with techniques, examples, real life scenarios, and resources designed to help you receive and live your life purpose.

This book has always been infused with the intent of guiding you in the rediscovery of your life purpose and learning to live your truth. We pray that you will embrace this intention as you progress through this book and in your own spiritual development. When infused with your loving intent, the techniques presented are powerful and are designed to increase your connection with both your divine self and Spirit.

This book is organized into ten chapters with each focused upon a different aspect of spiritual growth and development. Within these chapters, you will find prayers, spiritual requests, meditations, affirmations, and homework designed to create depth within the subject matter, an opportunity for practice, and the offer of spiritual assistance when needed. As you work through the meditations, you may wish to record them for yourself, have someone else read them to you, or experience the meditations Dr. Gale recorded and made available online. To access the pre-recorded meditations, please visit Dr. Gale's website at http://www.galeminchew.com/Meditations. Dr. Gale's meditations often blend guided imagery, hypnosis, visualization and affirmations for the greatest results possible.

Throughout the book, we interchange the words 'he' and 'she' when necessary. In an effort to protect the privacy of others, we have disguised the identities of those in the illustrated stories, except when the experience belonged to Dr. Gale or Karen specifically. It is our hope that you will relate to some of the stories presented and expand upon them by adding your own experiences as you move through the chapters.

We suggest that you purchase or dedicate a journal for this experience. You may wish to decorate it or formally dedicate it to this process in some way. Whatever you choose is just perfect for you. Remember, you are a unique soul perceiving and expressing everything you experience in your own, beautiful way. Allow your perfection to shine!

Like most material of this nature, this book is not a substitute for medical or mental health assessment and treatment. Instead, it is designed to assist you with rediscovering and fulfilling your life purpose. Because of the mental, emotional, and spiritual work you will accomplish while reading this material, we want to stress how important it is that you properly care for yourself.

Drink plenty of water while working through the exercises herein. It is important to nourish your cells and flush toxins from your system so healthy eating habits and regular exercise are just as important. It is not necessary to use any extreme diets or intense workout regimens. You may find that five small meals per day or three fully balanced meals work perfect for you. Likewise, going for a walk, taking the stairs at work, a gentle yoga routine, or dancing in your living room with the radio up like no one is looking are all perfect possibilities. Continue with any medical or mental health services you are receiving until such time that you and your treatment team determine whether any changes are necessary.

And finally, have fun with this book. Find enjoyment in the exercises. Appreciate the changes you are bringing into your own life. You are an amazing spiritual being, and you can accomplish anything. Accept the challenges your soul gives to you and be open to making decisions that could change your life forever. And remember, there is no wrong choice, only different choices leading to various paths which beautifully end with the same conclusion…to live, to learn, and to love in everything that you do.

Chapter 1

I Am the Light

We often hear your questions and the despair and frustration in your voice... What am I here for, what is my life about, what should I be doing right now? The question you are really asking is this, "What is my life purpose?" But what is a life purpose, what does that mean, you wonder, dwelling on why you don't understand, what you don't understand, and how will you ever figure this out? You have been divinely guided to this book to help answer those questions.

It is our goal to connect with you in a meaningful way as you read these pages. This book will guide you on a personal journey of insight and understanding as we help you uncover your life purpose, discover your strengths and hidden gifts, and fully connect with the divine being that is You.

We ask that you first connect to the purpose inside of you…your life purpose. In preparing you for this step, we have gifted you a Life Purpose Prayer. For now, we have separated the prayer into two parts, with Part I being presented in this chapter and Part II being presented in the next chapter. It is our hope that presenting material in smaller sections will encourage you to more fully engage with the exercises presented in this book rather than becoming overwhelmed or over-stimulated.

When you are ready, find a quiet place where you will be able to recite these words freely and uninterrupted. The words in this prayer have much power and will resonate with your soul even if you have doubts or are unsure about the use of prayer in your life. You will find that once you give prayer a chance, doubt will melt away and you will connect with this prayer in a profoundly meaningful way. So now, close your eyes, take a couple of deep breaths, slowly release each breath and allow yourself to relax before you begin.

Life Purpose Prayer Part I

Dear God,

I ask to be strongly put upon my path so that I do not miss the signs that I now ask to be given, signs that I am on the path to

2

my life purpose. I ask to connect to my path in a way that is easy for me to see. Please create for me a way to become that which I desired before incarnating here on Earth. Help me to give my heart to this mission. I know that I am subject to the spirit of the light as my breath is theirs, my life is theirs, and my council is theirs. Align me with my mighty powers to serve this light so that my heart is one with the light.

As I meditate on my consciousness, I ask that I may know my truth and that I may see my heart clearly. Where I have come off of my path please realign my purpose to match my desires, including my relationships, talents, gifts, understanding, and future plans. I call upon the Higher Angels to help me in yielding to the light, the truth of all that is. I ask that you fill me with the truth of my purpose.

Free me now from all attachments of fear so that my progress along this life path, and the relationships that I create during this journey, are set forth to serve only my highest good. Thank you for planting this seed of truth within my heart today that it may grow into the light, with my desires in sight, and my plans connected in truth.

~Amen

***

Prior to incarnating into this lifetime, you created a plan for what you wanted to experience. You chose who you would be, your parents, and your experiences based on the lessons you hoped to learn. You were the conductor of the symphony of your life. For many, this is a difficult fact to swallow. Why would I want myself to ever go through that terrible event, you might wonder…or…Who would ever wish illness or abuse upon the self or another like that?

Your soul is constantly evolving and growing, and the lessons of each lifetime build upon each other, much like rugged steps rising up to a glistening crystal castle. That crystal castle is the highest evolution of your soul, the steps leading up are but the lessons you have learned upon the way. As your lessons bring you closer and closer to the castle, you will begin to notice that it glows brighter and brighter with each step you take. The brilliance you witness is but a representation of you.

Because you are a child of light, a part of everything that is Divine, the light within and around you reflects back to you just as a mirror reflects that which stands before it. That glowing light represents you, everything you were, everything you are, and everything you will become. Your flame has always maintained a beautiful spark, but as you draw closer to your highest evolution, your flame begins to glow more pure and even more brightly than ever.

We have often been asked what it means to be a child of light. The answer is both simple and complex. Every being incarnated on this Earth is a product of spiritual light. At your core, like everything in existence, you are energy... light and vibration. Indeed, you are of the highest truth...Divine perfection. You are a creation of the one true light that initially sparked the beginning of everything. You are pure, a part of the oneness of all, every being, everything that exists, and you are one with the light of the Divine.

As a part of all that is, you decided to incarnate on planet Earth to advance your spiritual knowledge and facilitate your soul's purpose. It is at this time, being a child of light became complex. In an effort to accomplish your soul purpose in this lifetime, you dimmed your light upon entering this Earthly realm. You either chose to forget who you are in truth or decided to refute only portions of your true self so that you may learn the lessons chosen for this lifetime, uncorrupted by foreknowledge of your soul's journey.

With this veil drawn across your awareness, separating you from truth, you continue along your spiritual path. And like so many others, you may be unaware of the circumstances you decided to experience in this lifetime until you reach the point of renewed spiritual activation. It is during this activation, a part of spiritual awakening, that you are finally able to release the hold you have exerted over your inner light as you acknowledge,

5

remember, and reclaim the full essence of your soul and the full effect of your flame.

It is important to remember that you enter this world as a child of light, a tiny spark of the Divine, and eventually evolve into brilliant light as you grow and advance along your spiritual path, much as a child blossoms into an adult. Throughout life, you work towards finding your way back to the truth of your real self and towards rediscovering the powerful light you are in Spirit. As you reclaim what is rightfully yours, you begin to recall that you are one with the highest light, one with everyone, everything, and all that is within your very core.

It is this light you are meant to spread across the planet. You are both blessed to be here and a blessing to this place. You came forth to shine your light wherever there is darkness and to share that light everywhere you go. Every being you meet through purposeful or chance encounter is affected by your unique light.

Although it is true that everyone is a part of the Divine light and that we are all one, no one shines quite like you. You choose to share your light in different ways, for different reasons, and at different times as best meets your soul's needs. For example, there are moments in each lifetime when you may not allow your light to shine as brightly for some reason or other. Most often this is the result of dissonance between the ego and your life purpose. Perhaps the ego wants you to be wealthy beyond measure but the soul yearns only for a lesson in giving of self to others. For a time, the ego amasses extravagant amounts of material wealth but the soul feels incomplete. Your light glows dimly until you remember that you are a child of light and rediscover the purpose of this life and the purpose of your soul

From time to time, you may feel as if you get stuck along the way. You may worry that your light is no longer burning or that you are not on the path of your true purpose. Sometimes, you believe you are experiencing this on a small scale while other times you may worry you have wandered off your entire life path, both of which lead you to not being aligned with your true purpose. These misalignments can occur at any time and in any way.

A young woman we will call Anna experienced this in the context of a family situation. During a recurring issue of family conflict, Anna found that it took months to realign herself with her true purpose. Although it was tedious work and she had to consistently redirect herself to this purpose, once she began working towards realignment, Anna noticed that the light began assisting her immediately. She tried repeatedly to befriend her son's stepmother for the benefit of her child. For months this woman caused problems between Anna and her son's father, petty arguments and disagreements that could have been avoided.

For a time, Anna was at a loss as to how to ease the situation. She began to focus inward and practiced communicating with the

Divine. Anna created a personal prayer, much like the Life Purpose Prayer presented earlier in this chapter. Like our prayer, Anna asked for assistance with her life, her purpose, and guidance toward the path she should be following.

Almost immediately, Anna noticed the problems she experienced with her son's step-mother were getting worse rather than better. She was receiving what we will call "spiritual push-back" from negative energies tied to the other woman. In praying for resolution, Anna was guided to change the way in which she dealt with the situation. Instead of approaching the problem in the same way, being nice and extending friendship, Anna listened to her inner guidance and was surprised by what she heard.

The angels explained that this was a recurring pattern for the other woman, a pattern that Anna was not responsible for correcting. Rather than her angels and guides asking Anna to "just be kind" or "let it go" as she assumed they would suggest, Anna was instructed to cease interactions with the woman immediately. The angels assured her they would assist in completely removing the woman from her life, which eventually came to pass. Anna came to understand that when she was willing to listen to the guidance her angels suggested, solutions were found, burdens were lifted, and she was able to return to the path in life she was meant to take.

Because Anna followed her angels' guidance, she no longer interacts with her son's step-mother and understands that this is one of the relationships the angels wanted her to release. As the connection to negative energies was severed and the "spiritual push-back" was released, interactions with her son's father improved, as well. Over a short period of time, this realization allowed Anna more time, energy, and resources to concentrate on her life purpose and allow her own light to shine brightly in truth so that she may move forward on her own life path.

You may present with a situation similar to Anna's or one quite different. Regardless of the circumstance, setting your intention with prayer can assist you in eliminating harmful, hurtful, or negative experiences from interfering with the decisions you make, the light you shine, and the path you walk in life. Your intention can be anything and is most powerful when it is in alignment with your highest good and ultimately allows your inner light to shine.

Examples may include: Today for my highest good, I set my intention...

...to be placed upon my true life path.

...to repair my relationship with _____.

...to forgive myself for _____.

...to resolve the situation regarding _____.

...to discover my life purpose.

Whichever intention you set, be open to the guidance the angels provide to you, without demands, without expectation. In adhering to your own expectations, requirements, or specifications for how actions should be carried out, you create a disconnect between your request for assistance and the true spirit of guidance. When you set your intentions and pray for assistance with your life path, your life purpose, or problems you are experiencing in life, be open to whatever answers come to you, whatever Angelic direction you receive, in whatever form those solutions wish to take. Be open to the Divine. Be open to the light. Like Anna, you may be surprised by the guidance you receive.

Affirmations

For the next three days, we ask that you affirm the following:

I am a child of the light.

My path is bathed in purity and oneness.

I am one with the thoughts of God and the spirit of the light (Holy Spirit).

I give my heart to the light and embrace my brilliant and passionate future.

My future is safe because my light is bright and powerful.

Homework

Take a few moments to consider your thoughts and feelings regarding today's lesson. Record in your new journal anything that stands out for you, speaks to your soul, or a nudging that there is something in this lesson you need to revisit.

Chapter 2

My Mission Is Guided By Truth

As you begin this journey of understanding and the discovery of your life purpose, remember that your mission is always guided by truth. That is not to say you will always stay true to the easiest path available to you. There are many paths in life and all of them lead to the same place. However, you have free will to choose whichever path you want to follow at any point in time. Some choose the difficult path, some choose the easy path, and depending upon the lessons you planned for this lifetime, sometimes challenging tasks arise along whichever avenue you take.

Regardless of which path you have chosen, you are exactly where you need to be at this very moment in time. And while it may not seem to be the case, every experience you have encountered up to this point, in this lifetime and beyond, has prepared you for today. Each of those experiences, whether you deem them positive or negative, has provided instruction and valuable knowledge necessary for fully living in the light of your purpose. Taking the time to rediscover that purpose is one step in the journey towards fulfilling your mission in life. On that journey you will find that your mission is simple really...Live, Learn, and Love.

Take a few moments now to quiet your mind and calm your body as you prepare for Part II of the Life Purpose Prayer. Inhale several slow, deep breaths and allow yourself to enter a space of peacefulness. When you are relaxed and your mind is still, recite the following prayer:

Life Purpose Prayer Part II

Dear God,

I accept my true path and no longer fear the unknown. I wait for each mission as I know I am guided to do, and pray that my soul may accomplish the will of my Spirit for each mission that I complete. I ask that you correct the soul paths of all whom I need to be involved with in Spirit and in truth. I understand that previous relationships and plans may be cancelled in order to realign me with my true purpose. I understand that because I am more than I have previously realized, certain thoughts or thought patterns may be replaced to align me with my true purpose. I ask for your guidance in helping me live in balance, for I know that balance and truth are one. From this day forward, I walk in truth. Please allow this prayer to serve as a seal to connect me to the Divine and to keep me aligned with my highest and truest purpose.

~Amen

***

You may wonder how people get so far off their life purpose. How does one stray from the path that she believes will bring peace, security, and happiness? The answer is simple really…free will. As a human being, you have the ability to make choices, to decide what you want to allow into your life, whether it be relationships, situations, environments, experiences, or tangible things. This is called free will. You are influenced by your choices, upbringing, environment, people with whom you interact, and general circumstances in life. Interestingly, these influences can send many mixed messages and cause confusion about your mission in life. When this happens, you come out of alignment with the truth of your life and your mission…you forget your purpose.

But, the beauty of free will is this: You can change your decisions and your path at any time. The first step of change is to have a real desire to realign with your true purpose. You must have a willingness to ask for help even if you worry you do not deserve assistance, because in truth, everyone is worthy of spiritual help at every moment in his life.

It is also important that you are willing to shift your perspective, if needed. We have found that the best approach to keeping your feelings and thoughts in balance with your desire for heavenly guidance is to remember the importance of the Law of Attraction. Whatever you focus most upon, whatever you give thought to or dwell upon, whatever emotions you live within will be drawn to you in return. Thus, according to this Universal Law, negative thoughts, feelings, and beliefs lead to more negative thoughts, feelings, and beliefs. Changing the way you perceive, think, and feel will help you to more quickly recognize the guidance and signs you are receiving which will, in turn, help you realign with your life purpose.

Consider the experience of a young man we will call Jason. Jason lived in a cycle of perpetuating negativity. He dwelled on the disappointments in his life, the missed opportunities, and the age old belief that nothing "good" ever happens to him. A couple of years ago, Jason was passed over for a job promotion and was instead transferred to a junior position within a newly created, fast growing branch within his company. He saw this move as a demotion rather than an opportunity. Each day, Jason dreaded going to work. He failed to see the signs Heaven was giving him until he started working on his life purpose.

Eventually, Jason became frustrated with his perceived situation and decided that he needed a shift in his life. As Jason purposefully focused his awareness on improving his career, he shifted his perspective about the new position and was finally able to see it as a stepping stone to greater rewards within the company. Instead of viewing the new position as a demotion, he became aware of the signs around him. These signs led Jason to understand that he was being groomed to take on a leadership role within the new branch of the company with a foundation beginning at the ground floor that would provide him the credibility he needed to lead his new team. A shift in his perspective allowed the Law of Attraction to work to Jason's benefit rather than drowning him in a pool of negative thoughts and emotions.

We have heard many of you question why is it sometimes so difficult to hear the guidance you are receiving. You wonder why you feel unsure of yourself and of the messages and signs you receive. Some of you express doubt that there are any signs or messages at all and believe instead that perhaps you have been forgotten or ignored. We are here to assure you that this is not the case. Your heavenly guidance is always with you and has always been with you.

Signs and messages come in many forms. You may find feathers or pennies in unlikely places. You may hear a recurring song on the radio. You may see recurring number patterns on the clock. You may see butterflies, dragonflies, or hummingbirds several times in a day. You may hear a voice in your head, feel an emotion, or see an image representing what you should do in a particular situation. The best way to recognize the signs as they present themselves to you is to first ask for signs and messages from Heaven. Next, be open to recognizing and receiving them. And finally, ask for help interpreting these signs and messages if you are uncertain about their meaning.

The following meditation is intended to help you recognize and interpret the Heavenly signs you receive. When you are ready, you may read along with the following meditation, record it for yourself for future listening pleasure, or enjoy the pre-recorded meditation available online. Whichever choice you prefer is perfect for you in this moment.

Meditation: Recognizing and Interpreting
Signs From Above

Take a few moments to find a comfortable position where you will not be disturbed. Begin focusing on your breath as each inhale fills your abdomen and each exhale fully releases the breath. Continue focusing on your breath as you slip into a deepening level of relaxation. As you melt into this comfortable state, take a moment to notice the thoughts that enter your mind.

Continue breathing, allowing each thought to drift away, one by one. It is perfectly normal for thoughts to enter your mind. However, in this space, at this time, it is not necessary to dwell on those thoughts. Release them with the out breath and replace them with calm and peacefulness as you inhale, slowly and gently. Become aware of the tension leaving your body. Allow all thoughts, stress, negativity, and tension to leave your body now.

In your mind's eye, notice a door in the distance. This door will open you to an even deeper state of relaxation where you will be able to interact with your inner world and the higher realms, the realms of love and light. It is in this space you may ask for assistance in recognizing the signs along your path, you may discover signs that you have been given but paid no attention, or you may seek interpretation for signs you do not understand. In a moment, count along with me to the number ten as you reach a deepening level of relaxation, with each step you take towards the door.

One…taking slow, gentle breaths. Two…moving deeper and deeper into your inner world. Three…continue breathing with each step. Four…calm, peaceful energy flowing around you. Five…sinking deeper and deeper. Six…closer and closer. Seven…signs of the Divine begin to fill you. Eight…steady breaths. Nine…deeper still. Ten…you reach the door.

As you stand in front of the door, notice any signs that have begun to fill you. If you brought signs with you into the meditation, carry them with you as you walk through the door. Step through the door now, into a space filled with Divine white light and Angelic presence. Find a comfortable place to converse with your angels. Feel them coming closer as you present your signs for Divine guidance or as you ask for signs to lead you along your path in life. Take a moment now and ask, "What signs have I or am I receiving from the Divine?" Allow the answers from your angels to come in.

As the energy and love of your angels surrounds you, you may continue to ask any other question that remains. You may regularly find feathers or pennies or recurring number patterns in your daily life. "Angels, please help me understand what these messages mean for me and allow only truth to fill my heart." Allow any additional answers or wisdom to come in, as well.

Take a few moments to breathe in the love and energy of your angels before you go. Ask that the angels continue to provide you with signs and help you to understand them in your waking life. Now, walk back to the door and before you step through, thank your angels for their guidance.

As you return to your physical body, you will take with you all the knowledge and wisdom the angels have shared with you regarding signs in your life. At the count of three, you will return feeling refreshed, rejuvenated, and ready to continue your day. One…two…three. Open your eyes and recall all that you learned during this meditation.

***

Recognizing and understanding the signs you receive in life may take some practice. Do not be discouraged. God and the angels are always with you, ready to help and ready to guide you towards your ultimate truth. Over the next several chapters, you will be encouraged to continue practicing this skill.

Affirmations

For the next three days, we ask that you affirm the following:

I am aligned with my life purpose.
I live in truth now and always.
I clearly recognize and understand the signs and messages that Heaven is giving me.

Homework

Spend a few moments in quiet contemplation about the signs and messages you have received in your life. It may be a current situation or something in the past. The goal of this assignment is to practice seeing the signs you have been given. In your journal, record some of the messages or signs you have received.

Chapter 3

I Live In Balance and Harmony

When you pray to be placed on your path and then affirm
that you are on the path that is right for you, the universe cannot
help but conspire to put you in that desired place. It is likely that
new situations, experiences, and people will come into your life.
Likewise, some of your current situations, experiences, and
relationships may be removed from your life completely.

With these two actions, initially you may feel off balanced or
confused. This is normal as you are realigning with the spirit of
your mission in life. You will soon find that this initial
discomfort is replaced by joy and happiness as the process by

which your realignment with the light and your true purpose unfolds.

As you place your life in the hands of God, you place your trust in the Angels to right the wrongs currently in your path and help you accept that all previous experiences came from a place of learning rather than error. It is important for you to understand that everything that has happened in your life up to this point was for learning purposes. It was designed to help you along your path in some way; thus, there is no reason to belittle or berate yourself over past decisions.

It is possible that your choices and decisions may have led you in troubling directions or taken you down a difficult path wrought with painful challenges. Perhaps your lesson along the difficult path was intended to prepare you for something else along your soul's journey. Similarly, it is possible you were meant to exercise your free will if for no other purpose than the ability to do so.

Whatever the motivation, remember that everything in life happens for a reason, even if we do not understand that reason. Nothing happens by accident or coincidence. Consider how you happened upon this book. Perhaps you bought it for yourself, or maybe a friend gave it to you. It may have fallen off a shelf at a store you visited or you saw it lying on a table in the clinic waiting room. Regardless of the way it came into your life, you were guided to this book for a reason, not by chance. Once you accept that nothing happens by accident, you will begin to see the ease with which you are guided back onto the path of your true life purpose.

Everything in life should be in balance, including home, family, career, hobbies, relationships, and education. When you are balanced, you experience general feelings of well-being and a sense of equilibrium in your life. You possess a knowing that you have been healed in Spirit. Intuitively, you understand that your Spirit is whole, perfect, and one with God.

However, if you do not feel that your life is in harmony, you may experience any or all of the following symptoms:

Anxiety

Depression

Anger

Unhappiness

Confusion

Insecurity

Pain

Often, a cause for these feelings cannot be readily identified. If you are experiencing insecurity, for example, you may feel unworthy, unsafe, unloved, and abandoned by others and by your higher power. Your unhappiness may be prompted by a general sense of lack, negativity, chronic complaints, or burnout. Or, perhaps you feel a sense of confusion which may be expressed as self-doubt, disassociation from self, or difficulty making decisions.

Alternatively, you may feel as if people take advantage of your love and kindness and find that you are always giving of yourself. You may experience health issues or similarly, you may have been advised that you need to change your diet, begin an exercise routine, balance the minerals in your body, or take vitamins and supplements. It is also possible that your symptoms manifest as loneliness, increased or decreased appetite, a lack of trust in yourself, or a loss of interest in activities you previously enjoyed. On the opposite end of the spectrum, you may overcompensate for the disharmony in your life with expressions of excessive pride, selfishness, aggression, inflated ego, and high risk or self-harming behaviors.

For some, it is possible that you do not experience any of these issues but still feel a general sense of disharmony. It may appear in the form of disillusionment with life, dissatisfaction, or apathy. Unfortunately and to your detriment, the imbalances in your life may cause you to look outside of yourself for something, anything to make you happy when in truth, happiness can only be found within. When you stop focusing outside of yourself and begin looking within, you will find the balance and harmony returning to your life with relative ease.

At first, this endeavor may seem complicated. You may wonder about all the steps you will need to take and the effort you will need to devote to the task. You may worry that you do not have enough information or personal resources to make any noticeable difference. However, the fact that you are reading these words suggests that you have everything you need in this moment to begin the process of restoring balance and harmony in your life.

Bringing your life back into an equalized state need not be complicated. At first, you may become overwhelmed by your own thoughts and feelings which may require that you simply retreat and reconnect with your true self. This is especially true if you feel the need to rest more during the day or sleep longer at night. Some of you may feel an intense need to be alone for awhile. Do not become alarmed by the need to disconnect. It is simply your soul asking for your help in restoring balance into your life. It is almost as if your soul is asking for a break or a brief pause to recoup before you continue with your work.

It is also possible during this process to become overwhelmed by too many projects that no longer hold your interest. Similarly, you may feel exhausted by a friend who demands too much of your time. In these circumstances, removing yourself from the situation or saying 'No' should be enough to restore your equilibrium.

However, there may be times when you need more resources other than a break during the day or a simple 'No'. In more complicated situations or those where you are still unsure how to return to your natural state, ask Spirit to lead you. Expressing your heartfelt intention will help ease the burden and facilitate your return to a balanced and harmonious life. The following request is intended to help you with this process.

Spiritual Request: Balance and Harmony

Dear Archangel Chamuel,

I ask for spiritual balance so that I may be confident on this journey and be aligned with my truest purpose. I realize that I need guidance to improve my life and create harmonious relationships within my path. I ask to be balanced and directed in harmony now and in all ways. I trust and release myself unto this process now.

I know that Spirit is bringing balance into my relationships, my connections, and my purpose in this moment. Help me to be open and willing to see and implement all changes that I need to make. I ask that you fill me with love and peace so that I may remain in balance within the path that is most appropriate for me at this time.

Thank you for your love and guidance, Archangel Chamuel.

***

Mental Exercise

Following this request, take a few moments to sit quietly and reflect on your path. It is important to clear your mind and allow Spirit to fill you completely. You will begin to have thoughts and feelings about how to restore balance into your life. Do not think of an answer to any questions that may arise. Instead, have patience as the answers begin to fill your mind. Your answers may present to you as a picture or vision in your mind. You may hear a word, feel something instinctively, or simply know the answer to your question all of a sudden.

***

As you begin harmonizing various aspects of your world, you will find it easier to regularly maintain balance in your life as a whole. With every decision you consider, quiet your mind and ask, "Does this coincide with my life plan…is this part of my true path?" After contemplating these questions, if you are still unsure whether a choice is in accordance with your highest good and in alignment with your life purpose, you may need to reconsider the decision you are weighing.

Acknowledging that there is a spiritual balance in life will ensure that you are one with Spirit at every moment. Once you realign with your life purpose, the universe will conspire to keep you from everything not in alignment with your path. Likewise, everything that is in alignment with your life purpose will begin materializing.

Several years ago, before we knew each other and before Karen knew we would write this book together, she was given the concept of the Life Purpose Prayer. Although the version presented in Chapters I and II represent our collaborated efforts, it is true to the intent of the original prayer the Angels gifted to her.

After receiving this prayer so many years ago, Karen prayed fervently to realign with her life purpose. Unfortunately, she was not consciously prepared for this realignment and experienced unanticipated consequences. At the time, she was engaged to a man for whom she cared deeply. She was perplexed by the Angelic messages she received explaining that she and her partner would soon go their separate ways because he was not the right person for her. Karen initially felt shock and confusion with this message because she believed the qualities of this man would be perfectly compatible with her spiritual journey. Karen did not acquiesce when faced with this unwelcome message and continued to pray. Instead of praying to be placed squarely on her life path regardless of any obstacles or surprises that might arise, she chose to include her fiancé, as well. Despite all of the messages to the contrary, Karen was convinced he was 'the one' for her and that surely her prayers would be answered in the way she anticipated.

Like many, Karen was reluctant to admit that the universe was clearing out that which no longer served her to prepare conditions for the exact person who was truly in alignment with her soul purpose. Because of her enmeshment within this relationship, Karen had difficulty recognizing that her life was out of balance in this area and needed Angelic intervention.

As her relationship began to shift, Karen felt that her life was falling to pieces. As people, situations, and experiences began to change in unexpected ways, Karen did not immediately recognize that she was being guided to return to her natural state of balance and harmony. It took time for her to see that the changes encompassing her life were the necessary ingredient for removing disharmony and restoring balance as she moved forward in full alignment with her life purpose.

As Karen eventually discovered, it is okay to allow the challenges of life to become stepping stones in the journey of the soul. Doing so allows you to learn from your mistakes. You will find it helpful to do whatever is necessary to minimize the anger and frustration you feel with this process, as ultimately, it is for your highest good. Know that all things that you have experienced up to this point were put in place for the evolution of your soul and that there are no mistakes, only lessons to be learned.

As you work through this process, it is important to speak positively about yourself and others. You will find that negativity has no place in a balanced life. Sometimes when you are unbalanced, you may have a tendency to denigrate yourself or someone else. To belittle or berate anyone for any mistake that is or was made only sends negativity out into the world, much like the negativity of gossip. In rediscovering your life purpose, recognize that it is time to release gossip from your path as this is not a part of your journey. Indeed, gossiping is one of the worst forms of negativity because when you are pointing out undesirable aspects of another...you are truly pointing out undesirable aspects of the self that you see mirrored in someone else. Thus, not only does this negativity affect the person that is being gossiped about, it affects you and the entire collective consciousness as a whole.

Instead of falling into this trap, remain positive and realize that you have learned many lessons, and that you are now ready to receive balance in your life. Recognize that everyone on the planet is evolving and each soul experiences struggles of varying degrees and on differing levels along the way. No two souls are experiencing the same challenges, nor are we in exactly the same evolutionary stage as another.

Although each of us have unique paths and varying lessons to learn along this journey, we contribute our personal wisdom to the whole. Every lesson learned by you and by others is connected to the collective consciousness of all and becomes a collective wisdom, so to speak. As you become more balanced in your life, you will begin to notice that this wisdom plays an important role in this process. Wisdom comes from seeing the light in each soul, including your own, and inspiring that light to shine brightly. Thus, collective wisdom facilitates positivity and light which in turn inspires the soul, which then creates more positivity and light within you and the collective as a whole.

You may wish to enhance your ability to access this wisdom and connect with your own light. If you have your own technique, you may use it now or you may use the prayer we have included herein. The choice is yours.

Take a few moments to relax. Close your eyes, take a couple of deep breaths, and allow yourself to connect with the Divine. When you are ready, open your eyes and recite the Wisdom Prayer, either aloud or in your mind.

Wisdom Prayer

Dear God,

I ask for your heavenly guidance in accessing the wisdom that is available to all so that I may live my life in balance and harmony. Help me to see the light in myself and others so that I may focus on the positive in life and thereby reject negativity along my life path. If I should stray from my purpose and instead chose a difficult path, help me see the lesson within my experience so that I may return to the balance needed to fulfill my life purpose. Thank you for the love and compassion you give me during my difficult times and the encouragement and support of the Divine wisdom you share with all.

~Amen

***

As you perpetuate this cycle of seeing the light within others, so too will you see the light within yourself and increase balance within your life. As you increase balance within your life, so too do you increase your connection with the Divine. By placing your life in the hands of God, you are rearranging your goals, priorities, and perspectives to bring you into balance and alignment with your highest good…your life purpose.

Affirmations

For the next three days, we ask that you affirm the following:

I release all fear to receiving balance in my life.
I trust that I am able to maintain a Divine balance.
I trust that I will have an exceptionally harmonious life.
I have a balanced schedule and lifestyle.
I am confident in my divine balance.

I live in harmony with all who are in my life.

I create ways for my life to be harmonious.

Homework

Take a few moments to consider your best life possible. What are your passions, your dreams, your desires? What is it you most want to accomplish in your life? Contemplate what you would do differently with your life to bring it into balance. How can you place your life in the hands of God? Allow your passions to guide you. Record your reflections in your journal. Do not allow negativity to creep into your thoughts but rather, frame every statement positively as you practice the art of passionate writing.

Chapter 4

I Am Change

As you move through this process of opening up to your spiritual truth and aligning with all that is in your highest good, you may begin to recognize changes within yourself. Spirit communicates with you in many ways, offering unique signs and guidance along your journey. It is important to recognize and pay attention to the signs you are given. If you are ever uncertain about a sign you receive, ask Spirit to help you see and understand the signs meant for you. The following prayer is offered to connect you with the Divine as you set your intention for increased clarity in your everyday life, meditation, and the dream state so that you may become aware of and understand the messages Spirit is delivering to you through your own unique constellation of signs.

Signs of Guidance Prayer

Dear God,

I ask to see and recognize the signs from my spiritual guides and Angels that show me that I am on the right path. Allow me to see only the truth of life that I may embrace the security of my life purpose. I ask to be guided clearly, and I now release any fear of receiving this guidance. I release any fear about missing the signs that I must see. I embrace the team of spiritual guides that you have sent to assist me. I ask that they continue to help me recognize all signs meant for me and clearly see all that I am meant to see in each moment.

~Amen

***

As touched on above, there are as many different signs as there are beings in this world because we each perceive things from our own personal experiences and perspective. In Chapter 2, we mentioned feathers, pennies, and number patterns as possible signs you may receive from Heaven. Your signs and messages may come to you as a voice in your ear, a recurring thought, or an idea out of nowhere. Additionally, your signs may come in the form of visions that appear to you in your waking life, during meditation, or even within a dream.

A beautiful example of this was illustrated for Dr. Gale a few years ago. She received a referral to work with three young children who had recently experienced trauma. Their mother was killed which necessitated that the children move in with their grandparents. While the members of the family worked to share time with the children, help them through their pain, and put the pieces of their own lives back together, the grandfather and oldest child realized that they were seeing pennies everywhere. In comforting his granddaughter, the grandfather explained to her that these pennies were signs from Heaven…signs that her mother was saying hello. The young girl was comforted by this and enjoyed the pursuit of finding pennies wherever they went together.

We have heard similar stories from so many people with whom we come in contact. Chances are that you have also experienced something similar. Dr. Gale once questioned why she received counsel from the angels in her dreams but did not see the recurring number patterns that others saw. In discussing the matter with Karen, it was determined that not everyone receives the same signs in the same way. Because Dr. Gale received information in her dream state, it wasn't necessary that she receive signs in the form of recurring number patterns.

Like the physical signs, you may become aware of mental signs, like Dr. Gale's dreams. The presence of repetitive thoughts over a period of time is another example of the mental signs we are sometimes given. Perhaps your mind keeps coming back to a movie you need to watch. Once you view this movie, you realize the answer to a question you had been pondering was right there, playing out on the screen before you. Likewise, you may have repeatedly considered taking an alternative route to work but ignored altering your routine. Then, one day you tried that new route and found just the house you had been looking to buy. Or, maybe you have received a recurring message to give up on a situation that was not working for you, or the alternative, you are encouraged to go into a situation that you had previously thought was not in your best interest. However these repetitive thoughts present themselves, know that they are signs from the Divine urging you to take heed.

When we step back and remove our ego from the equation, it is much easier to recognize the signs as they present themselves in each unique thought and moment. It is true that this is not easy for everyone initially. You may need repetitive and consistent practice in setting aside the ego so that you can master the meaning and symbolism of the constellation of signs that your spiritual team is using to communicate with you.

In practicing and becoming more aware of the signs, you may observe that your feelings about certain people, situations or events are shifting. This very situation happened for the young woman, Anna, who we discussed previously. When Anna began her own process of increased self-awareness, she noticed that her feelings about her son's step-mother changed immediately. She could feel in her heart that this woman was not an asset to Anna's relationship with her son and that the woman's intentions were anything but peaceful unity.

As you become accustomed to recognizing and deciphering the signs Spirit is providing, you will begin to hear your inner voice and your own thoughts about your future. These thoughts and the guidance of your inner voice may differ only slightly or quite drastically than before. It is different for every individual, and truly there is no right or wrong manner in which you perceive this guidance. The only necessity is that you begin to recognize whether your perceptions are in alignment with your life purpose. Over time, this task will become easier, and you will not feel as if you are struggling to be in alignment with your true purpose.

Be patient with yourself during this process and know that your spiritual team will continue helping you develop and fine tune your gifts, including your ability to clearly see the signs along your path. You will begin to notice synchronicities in life, or co-occurring events that seem to draw your attention to a message, thought, action, behavior, or feeling.

These synchronicities can serve to take you places you never expected. While writing this book, Dr. Gale dreamt of a beautiful blue butterfly flitting in the yard before her. She took out her phone to take a photograph and the butterfly flew straight towards her and paused so that she could capture the image. Dr. Gale snapped two photographs before the butterfly flew away. Also during this time, Dr. Gale noticed butterflies playing in her yard on a daily basis. Further, as she scrolled through her news feed on a social media site, Dr. Gale found repeated postings containing butterflies. She immediately recognized this as a message and told Karen she thought this book should contain a blue butterfly on the cover. In doing so, Karen recalled a previous message she received from the angels that this book would have a butterfly on the cover. And in this synchronicity, the cover for this book was conceived.

Mental Exercise

Take a moment to look back on the past month. What signs, patterns, themes, or synchronicities do you notice? Do they seem to be in alignment with your life path?

***

One of the easiest ways to identify whether you are in alignment with your path is the occurrence of Divine timing. It will seem as if everything you come across in life is prepared just for you. You may feel a positive vibe letting you know that all is well. You may feel a newfound confidence in making decisions. You may sense that your next step is just right for you in this moment, and you will have the courage to take that step. Everything just seems to come together for you, like the pieces of a puzzle finally falling into place. Divine timing is the ultimate in synchronicities as all things conspire to align you with your true path.

As you may have noticed, alignment with your true path will likely require some changes in your life. While signs, themes, and patterns will alert you to the coming changes, synchronicities serve to confirm the messages you have received, and Divine timing serves to propel this change forward.

All change influences the structure of human life and allows you to move ahead. For, without change or movement you experience no momentum in life. When you remain upon a stagnant path, you cannot experience life at its fullest. This may cause unexpected feelings of sadness, discomfort, or listlessness to rise to the surface. However, once you recognize and fully embrace the concept that life is filled with change, you will begin to relax into these transformations and actually become change. It is change that perpetuates the momentum of life, and because of this, it is change you are meant to experience in this incarnation.

It is common to experience difficulties during times of change. As human beings, we tend to become accustomed to the way things are and often go through the motions rather than alter anything in our lives. We may tell ourselves that we will go with the flow because it just seems easier that way. We worry that change may elicit something negative in our lives.

However, this worry, fear, and apathy do not truly represent the spirit of change. As mentioned above, change is natural. It is a normal part of this Earthly experience. Because we are made of energy and everything in this world in made of energy, we are neither created nor destroyed. Instead, we are in perpetual change at all times, and our mental, physical, and emotional beings know this.

While it is true that much of the change in our lives is subtle or below the conscious level of awareness, often we still know it is taking place. The cells within our bodies change, our physical features change as we age, the flow of a river changes, our pets change their behavior in response to our actions, and we expect these changes. If all of this change is taking place within and around us, albeit often on a subconscious or unconscious level, it is logical that the conscious aspects of our lives are prepared for change, as well.

The following request is intended to offer support in the acceptance of change in your life. As the Angel of change, you may call upon Archangel Michael anytime you need assistance welcoming transformation of some kind into your life.

Spiritual Request: Welcoming Change

Dear Archangel Michael,

I ask for your assistance in releasing fear as I move forward in my purpose. Please help me recognize the natural state of all changes in my life and know that they are focused only on allowing the will of my heart, my highest self, and the will of God.

I acknowledge your presence in all of the circumstances, situations, and changes in my life. I know that you are influencing these changes for my highest good. Please help me to remember that I am not alone on my path and that my Angels and guides are always with me. I ask that you continue to comfort, support, and encourage me as I walk along my path.

I am change. I know this change allows me to remain steadfast upon my journey. Protect me from harm, ease my worry, and show me the truth at all times. I accept these beautiful gifts of change. I choose to remember this as I continue in peace along my journey. Where peace can abound, I ask that it abound. Where joy can be experienced, I ask that it be experienced.

Archangel Michael, I thank you for your continued love, support, protection, and encouragement as I welcome change into my life.

***

You will find that some change in your life comes about quite rapidly while other change takes place over a lengthy period of time. Some of you may struggle to understand the intensity of the changes that you experience within you and all around you. You may question yourself, others, or even God as to how these changes serve your highest good. While it is in our human nature to question, it is also in our nature to have faith and allow.

While change is inevitable, there are ways in which you can improve the process and usher in the transformations that will improve your life and place you on your path with ease. Of these, an attitude of grace is likely the most important. Gratitude for change will strengthen your ability to have joy in any situation and will bring in more light and guidance as you continue along your path. You may wish to offer a simple prayer of gratitude for the changes that have come or are coming into your life. Alternatively, you may wish to mentally list everything for which you are grateful in life. Another option would be to create a list, read it before you go to sleep at night, then place the list under your pillow so that your gratitude may permeate your dreams.

Patience is another way to bring about a more fulfilling sense of change into your life in general. As you progress through these changes and come into alignment with your truth, be patient with yourself. Affirmations and meditations can greatly assist with the development of patience. In order to maximize the benefits patience can offer you in all areas of your life it is helpful to purposefully practice patience on a daily basis.

Above all else, know that change is beautiful. It is the essence of your soul and it is the core of your Spirit. You are meant for change and change is meant for you. The beauty of change lies in the transformation of your being, in becoming who you are meant to be. Much like the caterpillar retreats to his cocoon to await his new path as a beautiful butterfly, so too do you await your own transition into an awakened being in alignment with truth on this spiritual journey we call life.

Affirmations

For the next three days, we ask that you affirm the following:

I am change.
I easily allow changes in my life.
My path is secure.

I am now aligned with the signs and messages necessary for my spiritual development.

I easily see all of the signs my spiritual team provides to me.

I welcome change into my life for my highest and greatest good.

Homework

In your journal, record the changes you observe in your thoughts and feelings. This is a great way to further your progress. It creates a natural conduit for connecting your thoughts with your desires. Keep your journal ready as revelations may come during the day or night. Be sure to record any dreams that stand out or those that seem repetitive in nature. Utilize the skill of automatic writing to ask questions about how you really feel about a situation, decision, or person with whom you've come into contact. This will enhance your inner guidance, and you will learn to speak your truth. During this exercise, do not think about your answers, just document them.

Chapter 5

I Release All That No Longer Serves Me

As your life begins to shift with the changes that are occurring within your heart and mind, do not fear what is coming. You will be called upon to release that which no longer serves you and to cut cords to everyone, everything, and every situation that is not in alignment with your highest good. Holding onto the past, your hurts, fears, misgivings, disappointments, or mistakes will only hinder your spiritual growth. Allow yourself to learn the lesson within each situation or relationship you have experienced then be willing to leave the past in the past.

Every time you connect with another person, energy cords of light are created. Whether it is in conversation or direct or indirect interaction with a family member, friend, acquaintance, or stranger, these cords attach to you for better or worse. They can range in size from thin cords to thick. These cords can be of pristine shining light or alternatively, they may have a murky, clouded appearance due to the negativity related to the trauma surrounding the relationship or situation involved.

These cords keep you attached to that negative person or situation even when you have ended all interaction or the other person has walked away. Allowing these cords to remain attached may cause you to feel drained, frustrated, depressed, angry, or anxious and can impair your ability to feel peace, security, and even the presence of your Heavenly Angels.

You may notice disruptions in eating or sleeping, a negative pattern of interacting with loved ones, or profound loneliness, for example. Interestingly, many of these disruptions are correlated with mental health issues such as anxiety or depression, prompting you to seek treatment and/or medication. Feelings and behaviors such as these may be a sign that it is time for you to step back and release the entanglements of the past.

Soon after Karen began realigning with her true purpose, she realized that her relationship with her fiancé was deteriorating around her. At the time, she did not see the humor in her situation, but in hindsight the crumbling relationship was so obvious it should have been clear. Karen found that those within her inner circle also believed the relationship to be on solid ground and were actually shocked by its collapse.

Years later, Karen is still amazed by how the light and her guides transformed the situation with her former fiancé and released her from that bond. Although she felt devastated at the time, looking back, Karen clearly sees that the relationship would not have been in her highest good, and that she would not be in the place she is today.

Mental Exercise

Take a few moments to consider any past relationships or situations that you are holding onto in some way. Try to suspend judgment for this exercise. With a clear mind ask yourself, "Do I need to release this person or situation?" Try to identify everything and everyone you need to release.

***

As the Angel of protection for all of mankind, Archangel Michael will assist you with this process, even when you are unsure who or what to release. When you call upon him for help, he will cut all cords that no longer serve your highest good. This action will detach detrimental or stagnant energy that is no longer in alignment with your life purpose. By cutting these cords, you are removing the attachment of anyone who creates problems in your life, any problematic situations, and any individuals who are no longer meant to accompany you on your life path.

Do not worry about your attachments to loved ones. Your attachments to your spouse or significant other, children, extended family, and friends are never severed as long as they are connections of love. The only cords Archangel Michael will cut are those that prove to be harmful to you in some way.

Some cords will be attached to both you and the other person or situation while others may be only attached to you. You will find that it is much easier to release someone when they have no cord of attachment holding you, as well. Regardless, when called upon, Archangel Michael will help with both types of attachment.

In addition, there are some cords, such as attachments to children and parents, which do not need to be released but may need to be purified. Dr. Gale has counseled with many individuals who needed just that…a cleansing of their attachments with a parent, spouse, or child. A recent case she worked involved a man and his teenage son. Over the years they seemed to have drifted apart with the father believing his son was spoiled and only wanted his way and the son believing his father only cared about himself. In working with the pair, Dr. Gale found that they were gradually building resentment towards each other and each failed to see the relationship from the other person's perspective. Unfortunately, the relationship was becoming toxic. Because of the nature of their relationship as father and son, and with no signs of abuse being the cause of the deterioration, Dr. Gale consulted the Angels and found that a cleansing of the attachment was in the highest good of both father and son. She determined that once the cords of attachment were purified, the father and son would be able to move forward with a healthier attachment built of mutual respect, understanding, forgiveness, and love.

The process of purification works to cleanse and detoxify any stagnant, negative, or toxic energy. Thus, purification of any cords of attachment that you are meant to maintain will clear them of any energy that is detrimental to you and your life purpose. Because of this, the purification process is not intended for any random connection or relationship that does not serve your highest good. It is only for those connections that will help you fulfill your life purpose.

Like every decision that presents itself to you, you have free will choice. It is now time to consider whether you are willing to cut the cords of everything and everyone that no longer serves your highest good or whether you choose to keep these cords attached. Cord cutting is a powerful process and may produce results that you had not anticipated, such as people, circumstances, and emotions being removed from your life. Thus, a conscious decision is necessary moving forward.

When you make the decision to cut these cords, there is no formal process that must be undertaken. It is sufficient to use your words or voice to request that these cords be severed. In doing so, you signal your agreement for this action to be performed on your behalf. But remember, the Angels will not violate your free will in this situation. If you decide you are not ready for this process, you may skip the following meditation until a later time. But please understand, it is necessary for you to remove unhealthy attachments as you evolve spiritually and as you come into full alignment with your life purpose.

When you are ready to proceed, guide yourself through the following meditation. You may find it helpful to record the meditation for yourself, have someone read it to you, or access the pre-recorded version available online. Whichever choice you decide upon is just perfect for you at this moment in time.

Meditation: Cord Cutting with
Archangel Michael

Find a comfortable position where you will not be disturbed for the next few minutes. Allow your eyes to gently close as you concentrate on your breathing. Take several slow, deep breaths as you allow your body to sink deeper and deeper into complete relaxation. Allow any thoughts that may come into your mind to simply drift away as if on a breeze. They are not important at this time. This time is meant for you. Allow any external noises to lull you into a deeper state of relaxation as you prepare to call in Archangel Michael.

Now, imagine yourself as a large tree with many branches. These branches represent all of the cords that attach you to other people and situations. Most of these branches are long and beautifully curved with leaves of every shade of green. As your eyes dance from branch to branch, you notice that time and adverse conditions have taken a toll on some of your branches. You see now that some are twisted and broken as if they had been caught up in a storm while others are darkened or spotted as if traumatized by toxins or disease. As a healthy tree, you realize it is important to remove the branches that are no longer thriving and fruitful.

Knowing that you may ask for assistance with any area of your life, you call upon Archangel Michael now. "Archangel Michael, please wield your mighty sword of light to cut away any branches that no longer serve my highest good." Watch as the damaged branches fall away one by one and feel the freedom of release from each toxic relationship or situation they represent. Notice that Archangel Michael has removed these branches to a clearing located a safe distance away from you. Allow a flame of purity to engulf the cut branches until nothing remains but the transmuted energy of love.

As you observe the flame of purity, feel the healing energy of Archangel Raphael joining you now. Notice a glowing, healing rain of light wash over you as you are cleansed of any stale energy. Feel your burdens lighten as you are cleared of all things that no longer serve your highest good. As this rain of light falls upon you, feel a wave of purity sweep over you, cleansing all attachments that still remain. Feel the vibrancy in your core extending out to your healthy branches. Feel the blessings, love, and healing that surround you now.

Before you return to continue your day, thank Archangels Michael and Raphael for their love, protection, and healing. Watch as they ascend to join the healing light that only moments ago purified your remaining connections. Feel the new found inner strength that fills you now. When you are ready, open your eyes, feeling lighter and free from the burdens of unhealthy attachment. It is time. You are now awake, alert, and energized for the day ahead.

***

In an effort to insure that all negative attachments have been removed, it is beneficial to repeat this meditation once a day for the next week. You may wish to revisit this meditation from time to time after that period to remove any new negative relationships or adverse situations that present in your life or to sever any stubborn energy cords that may have reattached over time.

The power of your imagination knows no boundaries. You can release negativity and heal wounds simply by imagining that it is done. It does not matter if you know what cords have been cut or situations have been released. The only thing of importance is that you set your intention for serving your highest good and know that this action is now complete.

Affirmations

For the next three days, we ask that you affirm the following:

I release all people, situations, beliefs, and things that no longer serve my highest good.
I am now released from the detriment of negative energies.
I am free to engage and help those whom I wish to help.

Homework

Drink plenty of water and take time to rest following the release of negative cord attachments. In your journal, record any insights you received from your meditation.

Chapter 6

I Reject Past Life Limitations

You may feel that cutting cords did not seem to work as well as you expected. Instinctively, you may feel that it simply was not enough. When this occurs, it is likely that cords are not the only thing holding you back from your life purpose. Rather, it is possible that your past has become entangled in your now. We are speaking of your past lives, each life you have lived before this current lifetime. Some of us have had many past lives while others have reincarnated upon this Earth only a few times. In each of these lives, our experiences are meant to be lessons from which we learn and grow spiritually.

When we incarnate into a new life, we are meant to begin as a blank slate, ready to embrace the experiences we chose prior to incarnating. Sometimes, this becomes complicated when we return to the Earthly plane for a new human experience. Instead of incarnating as a blank slate, we end up carrying over limiting thoughts and beliefs into this new lifetime.

While you do not intentionally bring this baggage along, it weighs heavily upon your heart and inhibits your spiritual growth, causing kinks in the plans you had created for this lifetime. It is possible that you carry burdens from the renunciation of spiritual abilities in a past life, a carryover of past life vows, or unnecessary contracts from your life between lives.

For example, it is common to find that people who were healers in a past life often relinquish their spiritual abilities for future lifetimes. But, what could prompt a soul to reject an innate aspect of itself? Unfortunately, it is often the result of fear or coercion.

Historically, certain religious groups looked down upon natural healing, spirit communication by the lay person, prophecy, and so-called fortune telling. Anyone practicing these skills might be indicted for witchcraft or heresy, for example. Something as simple as offering herbs to a villager with an ailment could create great distress for an innocent practitioner of ancient homeopathic healing.

Interestingly, although many Biblical figures received visits from Angels and Spirit, for centuries it was consider sacrilege for the common person to think they were worthy of reciprocal communication with a higher authority other than the church. It is widely known that Joseph prophesied through dreams; politicians worldwide, such as former U.S. President Ronald Regan, rely on psychics for knowledge of the future; and farmers across the globe consult an almanac or wisdom from the elders to intuit profitable planting seasons, and have done so for generations. Unfortunately, over the history of humanity it has become clear that those who suggest they can prophesy or communicate with Spirit have long been criticized despite the common thread running through the fabric of our ancestry...these abilities are innate and a natural part of our soul.

Consider the Salem, Massachusetts witch trials of the late 1600s or the European witch trials between the 15th and 18th centuries. Many healers during these times were ordered to renounce their beliefs, tortured, burned at the stake, hung, or drowned because of their spiritual abilities. By the 1700s, several courageous scientists began evidencing proof that spiritual abilities exist but quickly found themselves ostracized from or shamed by the greater scientific community.

This was a very dark period of our evolution as a collective, but a time we needed to experience for reasons only our souls fully understand. Because of the threat of harm and actual injury inflicted upon people, many souls renounced their spiritual abilities during these lifetimes in the hope that they would be spared the pain or chastisement and would never be hurt again. This is a strong renunciation built upon strong emotional reactions, and for many, it has carried over from lifetime to lifetime.

With this in mind, it may seem clear to some of you that you have forsaken your own spiritual abilities because of a lifetime in which you were persecuted as a healer. While this refusal to acknowledge your true nature may have seemed to be an appropriate measure of self-preservation at the time, it has become an unnecessary burden as you travel upon your spiritual path.

Fortunately, even though this detrimental belief system may have carried over into this lifetime, you may ask that your spiritual gifts be returned to their rightful place…within your heart. It has never been wrong for you to have spiritual gifts. If you believe you have relinquished your gifts, or if you are not certain but wish to engage with Archangel Michael to find out, let us do so now. To begin this process, find a quiet place where you can have a few moments to yourself. Take a few deep breaths, close your eyes, and relax so that it will be easier to go within. When you are ready, open your eyes and recite the spiritual request aloud.

Spiritual Request: Reinstate Spiritual Gifts

Dear Archangel Michael,

I hereby remove all requests that I may have made in any lifetime that limit my spiritual gifts in any way. I release to myself my full range of spiritual gifts and request that they immediately be incorporated into my being. I now accept each of my gifts as they come forward into my consciousness. I give myself permission to see them, interact with them, and use them in all ways for my highest good. I thank the Divine for these gifts and will only use them in the highest light.

Thank you for your love and protection, Archangel Michael.

✹ ✹ ✹

In addition to rebuking spiritual gifts in a previous lifetime, some people take on past life vows. Vows can be a binding force within the belief system of humanity. You have agreed to many past life vows through the course of your soul journey and for each lifetime they serve an important purpose.

A vow may be an agreement to serve a specific role such as a family member, teacher, helper, lover, friend, boss, servant, or any number of other relations to some other person in your life. Sometimes this vow is a simple promise made to a child...I will love you forever or I will always take care of you. It may be a promise you made to your spouse…I will never leave you. These vows can resurface lifetime after lifetime, and you may feel that you cannot say 'No' to anyone.

These vows may also have manifested in the form of vows of poverty, celibacy, chastity, self-sacrifice, silence, suffering, and obedience, for example. All of these may have been appropriate for you in that lifetime, but in this lifetime, they no longer serve your highest good. It would seem these vows should end when that lifetime ends, as each soul is meant to begin each new lifetime with a clean slate.

From time to time however, lingering traces of those vows carry over into the current lifetime causing a variety of problems in relationships, love, finances, career, beliefs, thoughts, and behaviors. In limiting your access to the gifts that belong to your soul and disrupting your prosperity, health, and happiness, these vows deny you the very abilities that are integral to your spiritual evolution.

Thankfully, it is not difficult to discover the effect these vows may have exerted over your life. Past life vows carry with them a heavy burden that can be identified within the chakra system and easily understood using the principles of each chakra. The energy centers within the body correspond to different vows depending upon the area of life they affect.

For example, vows of poverty correspond to the root chakra, the energy center responsible for our basic needs of survival.

You may struggle with finances or feel that you never quite get a step ahead. Or alternatively, you may gamble away or waste your money as an excuse for never having enough. Vows of poverty may cause serious disruption to the root chakra and result in an experience of lack in your life and never being able to meet your basic needs.

A vow of chastity corresponds to the sacral chakra, the center of sexual energy. Often, those who have taken this vow discover that they have difficulty with intimacy or a lack of sexual desire. They may have problems conceiving a child or experience sexual dysfunctions that serve to excuse the sexual imbalance altogether. This interference with sexual energy, as a result of a vow of chastity, can lead to seemingly irreparable and significant distress in intimate relationships.

Vows of self-sacrifice correspond to the solar plexus chakra, which is the basic core of the self, how you identify yourself, the ego, and the personality. Those who have taken this vow typically sacrifice personal needs for the needs of others. They also tend to predicate their self-worth on their level of self-sacrifice. If you have taken a vow of self-sacrifice, it is likely that you put others needs ahead of your own to the detriment of your own physical, mental, or emotional well-being. In addition, you may feel drawn to help everyone with whom you come in contact to the exclusion of your own needs. This vow greatly affects the way in which you view yourself and subsequently the energy you express to others about your identity.

In continuing this theme, the heart chakra may be compromised by vows of celibacy, which dictates a separation from others and difficulty with expressing love. This vow suggests that you have chosen to refrain from giving love to an intimate partner in this lifetime. Often we see this vow evidenced in those who join the priesthood, nunnery, or monastery, although not every case of devotion to the Divine is due to dysfunction within the heart chakra. For those who have taken vows of celibacy, they may notice a disruption in the heart chakra which can be identified by failed intimate relationships and a fear of commitment. This jeopardizes the ability to express love to another and increases the likelihood of jumping ship when the moment of commitment draws near.

Difficulties with the throat chakra often correspond to a vow of silence. Since the throat chakra is the energy center of communication, those who choose not to engage with others in verbal communication or those who deny their own truth may experience blockages in this energy center. Fear often prompts this imbalance. Unfortunately, those who are fearful of speaking the truth about their beliefs have been silenced over lifetimes. Their pain and discomfort has endured and managed to accompany the soul in the most recent incarnation in the form of silence. This silence hampers the spiritual evolution of all souls as we collectively endure strife and misunderstanding through a lack of communication about the spiritual self.

A vow of suffering often correlates to a blockage within the third eye chakra. A disruption in this energy center can be quite toxic and lead to self-harming behaviors or allowing harm to come from others. Those who take a vow of suffering may remain in abusive situations, may engage in harmful behavior such as self mutilation or starvation, or find themselves repeatedly waiting for punishment for some perceived infraction. Ultimately, imbalances in the third eye chakra disrupt your ability to intuit information and use your extra sensory perceptions to engage with the world around you.

And finally, it is also possible that you brought into this lifetime a perpetuating vow of obedience, experienced within the crown chakra. Those who have given up their own will, and instead submit to the will of another, may notice an imbalance in the crown chakra. You are made of free will. To blindly follow another or lead others under a false premise of obedience effectively gives away your power, your will. Many people living under vows of obedience struggle with self-esteem, perhaps thinking they are not good enough, not strong, cannot make it on their own, and do not know where to turn. Unfortunately, false leaders tend to prey upon these individuals, for they have found that it is much easier to exact submission and deference to that leader's will than to engage with individuals who exert free will and a balanced crown chakra.

Because past life vows can significantly impair your spiritual growth, it is necessary to take steps to remove these vows and return to a more balanced state of being. Let us take a few moments to ask Archangel Michael for assistance. Again, find a quiet place where you can have some time to yourself. Take a couple of deep breaths, close your eyes, and relax so that it will be easier to go within. When you are ready, open your eyes and affirm the spiritual request aloud.

Spiritual Request: Releasing Past Life Vows

Dear Archangel Michael,

I ask to release all past life vows that I have made or that others have made on my behalf regarding anything that no longer serves my highest good. On behalf of my children, I break all vows that I may have made for them in a previous lifetime. I ask to be released from all effects of these vows…past, present, future, now, and forever. I release all belief systems tied to these vows through all space and time.

I ask for the complete removal of all limiting belief systems and those beliefs systems that do not serve my highest good or my life purpose. I release all fear and anxiety that may inhibit me from seeing the future and knowing the full scope of my spiritual abilities.

I ask to be reconnected to the bond of my own light. I humbly forgive all who have placed vows upon me or required me to take vows in a past life. I release all present vows that do not serve my highest good in this lifetime.

I trust that the light will guide me as I release vows related to people, situations, and beliefs that need to be detached from me. I ask for protection of my health, happiness, and safety as these vows dissolve.

Thank you for your love and protection, Archangel Michael.

***

In addition to relinquishing your spiritual gifts and holding onto past life vows, you may be carrying contracts that you made in your life between lives. During the between lives state, we review the life we just left and prepare for the life to come. The soul will evaluate where it is in its evolutionary process, as soul growth is an important step along our spiritual journey, and the soul will develop a plan for our next incarnation to include: what lessons need to be learn, what karma needs to be resolved, and what wounds from a past life need to be healed.

During this life review and evaluation of your soul's progress, you make contracts for your next incarnation. These contracts may include the conditions of your birth, your parents and family members, important life events that will present as lessons for soul growth, and significant others who will play a role in your life. In addition, you may be infused with unconscious information to help recognize significant others in your new life, those you have contracted with to learn your soul lessons.

Some of you may have contracted to marry a specific individual, have a certain soul as a child, or be exposed to significant health challenges or poverty, for example. Others may have chosen the experience of multiple failed relationships, being unable to conceive a child, or life of wealth and adoration. Whatever the contract, it was intended to help your soul grow and evolve.

Unfortunately, some of your life contracts are made without the benefit of the cumulative effect of all of your life experiences. It is true that you were shown the possibilities that may arise given the conditions your soul wished to experience. However, as most of you already know, sitting behind a desk making decisions based on information presented to you is much different from being out in the field making daily life choices and split-second decisions.

It is those contracts which end up impairing our soul's development that are of issue, not every contract formed between lives. Many of your contracts are exactly as they should be. And truthfully, most contracts should not be dissolved because they were made with careful deliberation for a specific goal, a certain lesson that needed to be learned, or karmic debt that needed to be fulfilled. However, if you believe the contract you have made is detrimental to your spiritual growth or is taking you off of your life path, you may ask the Angels for guidance and seek direction from the Divine.

The following prayer is designed to assist your with the discovery of any unhealthy soul contracts you may have made prior to incarnating in this lifetime. Be open to receiving this Divine guidance for the purposes it is intended. Relax and open your heart as you recite this prayer. And above all, be receptive to your spiritual guidance within.

Soul Contracts Prayer

Dear God,

I ask for your guidance now in showing me the true nature of my soul contracts in this lifetime. I do not come to you for pity or generosity, but rather as a student of my soul. At this time, I ask that you help me see my soul contracts in the context they were intended. Please guide me as I compare these intentions to the reality I am living.

Please allow my spiritual team to guide me in releasing these contracts if they are no longer serving my highest good or fulfilling the obligations they were intended to fulfill when my soul agreed to them between lives. For those contracts which are creating an undue burden on my spiritual development, please allow me to release them now if it serves my highest good.

~Amen

***

This prayer is quite powerful but is not intended to immediately remove contracts from your life. It is a great responsibility you must take on when removing soul contracts. Once you recite this prayer, be open to receive the guidance that your spiritual team and the Divine will continue to provide over the coming days.

You may not have an answer in one day or one week, and it is possible that you may need to recite this prayer from time to time to revisit the request for additional information about your soul contracts. This prayer is intended to give you a means for gathering additional information before you make a determination to release a contract rather than asking for that contract's release in this moment.

By heeding the guidance offered you after reciting this prayer, you will discover whether there are contracts in your life that may be released. Only after you determine that a specific soul agreement can be released based on the guidance of your spiritual team and the Divine, you may issue a simple request to dissolve that contract now, for your greatest good, and in all directions of time and space. We will discuss soul contracts more in depth in Chapter 9.

Affirmations

For the next three days, we ask that you affirm the following:

I fully release myself from all vows of the past that no longer serve my highest good.

I release all connections and vows from my past life family members in all directions of space and time.

I lovingly release and forgive all past life energies that I am detaching now.

I am happy to reclaim all energy that was taken, willingly or unwillingly, from me as I made these vows in any lifetime.

I am happy to release these vows, and I know that I am fulfilling my life purpose by doing so.

Homework

Take a moment to consider the vows you have released in this chapter. In your journal, record any thoughts and feelings you experienced as a result of the severing of these bonds. If you believe you have soul contracts or any other persistent past life limitations that may need to be released, record them in your journal so that you may revisit this topic for continued guidance.

Chapter 7

I Reject Fear

Fear is an illusion. Although we give it the ability to completely derail us from our desires, it is a creation of our own minds, the ego. We give fear power over us. We have learned to use it as a crutch. In prehistoric times, fear served an important role of self-preservation. And because of the collective consciousness that we share, fear of dangerous things and situations has perpetuated through the ages and kept humankind alive. Fear of the dark kept people in the Paleolithic Era safe from predators that roamed at night, for example, and fear of heights likely prevented our predecessors from falling off cliffs.

Somewhere over the centuries, the fears our ancestors used for self preservation from dangerous situations seem to have evolved into the irrational fears and phobias that are rampant in society today. Fear of flying, bats, rejection, heights, confined spaces, open spaces, failure, spiders, and an ongoing list of others, some with their own technical names that most of us do not understand and certainly cannot pronounce. But, these fears are not real. They are not created from a place of love. It is a means for the ego to trick us, to have control over the soul, and to hold us back in some way from moving forward in life.

For many, this includes fear of living one's life purpose. At a soul level, we instinctively know what our life purpose involves. However, when the ego becomes involved, we tend to over-think, criticize, and allow fear to creep in. Some people procrastinate or fail to act on their life purpose, while others make only half-hearted attempts and justify the ego's manipulation to sway them off the path, sometimes indefinitely. Common negative self-talk includes:

I'm not ready.

What if I can't do it?

I don't have enough (money, time, resources).

What if I'm rejected?

I'll do it later.

I'm not good enough.

Allow us to introduce you to Laura. She had always wanted to be a mother, even as a young child herself. Over the years, Laura evolved as a housewife and mother with healing abilities. But, Spirit wanted more for her. A few years ago, Spirit began guiding Laura to open a healing practice. She was unsure of this guidance and insecure with herself, not believing that she could create a healing practice on her own. As a result of her uncertainty, Laura decided to bear more children to put off making a decision about her life purpose. Her ego rationalized that if she was busy raising young children, she would not have time to own a healing practice.

Not too long ago, Laura realized that she was sabotaging her mission for this lifetime and that alignment with her life purpose was inevitable. However, she was unsure how to get her life back on track with her purpose. Laura was guided to follow many techniques similar to those presented in this book and made a deliberate choice to move forward with her life purpose. Today, Laura views this pivotal moment as a clear, conscious decision to follow her life plan.

It is important to remember that even if you doubt that you will be put upon your path or able to discover your life purpose, the universe will conspire to make this happen as long as it is your request. Set your intentions to align with your life purpose. Give your fears and doubts to the Angels so they may be transformed into positive energy. Allow everything that comes into your life or is removed from your life to help you realign for your highest good. Be patient with yourself as feelings of doubt and uncertainty begin to fade. You will find that over time, you feel more connected to the outcome of your life and begin to work together with Spirit to fulfill your mission. In time, you will be ready to understand and accept the truth that has always been within you.

If you find that you struggle with fear or have irrational fears that keep you from fulfilling your life purpose, you may wish to use the following meditation to help you align with your true self, abolish fear, and take back your power. When you are ready, find a comfortable place where you will not be disturbed for a few minutes. You may wish to record this meditation for yourself, have someone read it to you while you relax, or listen to the pre-recorded meditation available online.

Meditation: Releasing Fear with Archangels Michael and Uriel

Find a comfortable position and allow yourself to begin to relax as you take several slow, steady breaths. As you inhale, breathe in relaxation. As you exhale, breathe out all stress, tension, or worry that you may be carrying with you at this time. Notice as you relax deeper and deeper, you begin to melt into your surroundings. The seat or bed beneath you feels soft and welcoming. Sink further into this space with each breath you take.

As you become more and more relaxed and peacefulness begins to envelope you, take a moment to call upon Archangels Michael and Uriel. My dearest Archangels Michael and Uriel, I ask that you join me now as I work towards releasing fears and reconnecting with my power so that I may realign with my true self. I ask you to guide me on this journey and stay by my side as I complete each of the exercises asked of me.

Feel the loving guidance of Archangel Uriel as he comes in to stand by your side. Allow his brilliant golden light to completely surround you as his inspiring energy fills this space. Now, feel the presence of Archangel Michael standing before you with his flaming blue sword of protection. Allow his protective energy to wash over you as you prepare for the work ahead.

Take a few moments to breathe in this beautiful energy as Archangel Uriel hands you a book. Take the volume from his hands and notice how it changes to the perfect color and texture that pleases you. As you hold this book in your hands, feel the texture and weight of its paper. You gently peruse the treasures within, curious about what you have found. As you slowly turn the pages, you notice dark splashes of ink, making it difficult for you to see the images and words on each page. Archangel Uriel moves closer by your side and sends waves of calming energy throughout your being. In this deeply peaceful state, you take a seat and continue to leaf through the book, wondering, "What is the point when I can't see what is really here?"

You begin scanning the content that is visible on the page, but quickly find that it only tells part of a story…a story that you now realize is your life. Curious about this life story, you ask Archangel Uriel why there are splotched of ink in your book and how they apply to you. Archangel Uriel sits down beside you as you turn the pages. With his loving guidance, he helps you see the fears you have held throughout your life which have been recorded in this book.

With Archangel Michael standing ready to protect you from all harm, Archangel Uriel asks you to visualize each fear, feel your reaction to it, and know how it has affected your life. See those fears in the ugly, irregular splotches of dark ink on the page. One by one, look at each splash of ink and feel each of the fears they represent. Remember instances in your life when each of these fears has kept you down, minimized you, or derailed you from your path in some way. Take time to do this now.

Now, imagine each of the dark spots shifting upon the page, obscuring your view of your true life path, your true self. Archangel Uriel asks, "Do you want to see what is beyond the darkness?" Take a moment to consider your options. It is always your choice, your free will. Do you choose to live with your fears and obscure your life path or do you choose to release your fears and live in truth?

When you are ready to proceed, ask that Archangel Uriel show you the truth that is your life purpose. Archangel Uriel takes out a golden pen and as he places the tip near the page, you observe the ugly, irregular blotches of ink being sucked up into the pen, as if Archangel Uriel is un writing your history, removing your fears, releasing from the pages of your book anything that has blocked you from your true path.

Feel the burden of fear being lifted from your shoulders now. Feel the weight being lifted from your heart as you begin to see your true self on the pages. Feel your power. Know your power. Stand in your power now as you look at the shining pages before you.

You turn the page and see the words 'Life Purpose' written in elegant writing at the top. Below it, you notice a few words but realize this next chapter has not yet been written. It is a blank slate, ready for you to decide how you want to proceed. You look to Archangel Uriel for guidance and he explains, "Your path is now ready for you. It is time for your soul to write the next chapter, Dear One."

You smile in understanding and thank Archangels Uriel and Michael for leading you on this inner journey and safely clearing the path for you to begin the next chapter in the book of your life. As their energy ascends to Heaven, you revel in the energy they left behind, as a gift for you on this journey. When you are ready, you may gently open your eyes and return to the present moment feeling relaxed, rejuvenated, and empowered to continue the process of rediscovering your life purpose.

***

This is a powerful meditation and it will likely be necessary for you to drink plenty of water as the fears you identified continue to release over the next several days. Think of this chapter as detoxification of your mind, body, and spirit. Some may process this work easily, while others may feel quite sensitive or emotional. However you experience this work is perfectly appropriate. You are a unique soul and perceive and express in ways different from anyone else. Allow yourself to just be. If you notice more fears coming to your awareness, allow them to surface, feel them, and then release them into the light so that they may be transmuted in loving energy and released back into the world.

You may need to revisit this meditation in a couple of weeks to address any stubborn fears that are trying to hold on. In addition, you may choose to repeat this meditation from time to time to remind yourself to release fears and strengthen your connection with your personal power and life purpose. You are strong. You are powerful. You are fearless.

Affirmations

For the next three days, we ask that you affirm the following:

I am in alignment with my life purpose.

I make clear, conscious choices on my life path.

Everything I need to fulfill my mission comes to me in the
perfect time and manner.

I am strong.

I am powerful.

I am fearless.

Homework

Take some time to journal about your meditation experience
today. Record any fears that needed to be released. Search your
heart for any lingering fears that you will need to release at
another sitting.

Chapter 8

I Release Unhealthy Spiritual Contracts

In Chapter 6, we asked you to release all past life limitations. It is important to your overall spiritual development to release everything you no longer need and everything that no longer serves your highest good. Sometimes your limitations do not originate in a past life, however. In each lifetime and between lifetimes you enter into contracts and partake in vows that you believe are in your best interest. Just as you have done in past lifetimes, you have created agreements in and for this lifetime, as well. Unfortunately, these agreements do not always remain consistent with your highest good.

In this lifetime, you may have agreed to care for your brother's children in the event of an accident. You may have taken an oath in front of the church such as marriage vows or ordination. You may have signed a contract on a new home or verbally agreed to pay off all of your boyfriend's previous debt. Or, you may have promised God that if he will just make this one thing happen, you will never ask for anything again in your life.

Contracts and vows for this lifetime are initiated before we ever begin this life and are called spiritual contracts. As explained in Chapter 6, prior to incarnating, there is a period of review where you look back over the life you just departed and decide what lessons you want to learn and what experiences you want to gain in the next life.

During this review period, you may have agreed to conceive a child espousing the soul of a member of your soul family. You may have entered into a contract with another member of your soul family to help you learn a specific lesson that may present some hardship. Or perhaps you arranged to live within certain conditions and experiences during this lifetime that now seem unbearable. These are all spiritual contracts you agreed to fulfill prior to coming into this life.

Spiritual contracts are important for your growth and should not be retracted without serious consideration. However, if you feel that there is a contract that is preventing you from fulfilling your life purpose or one that places you in an abusive situation, you may request that the contract be removed and revoked. Your work in Chapter 6 should have prepared you for this possibility.

For example, before you were incarnated you may have made an agreement with another soul, but over time that soul may have changed into an abusive person who is no longer in alignment with your highest good. It is faulty thinking to believe that you are meant to be used and abused by anyone in any lifetime. Because of this, it is possible an adjustment may need to be made. Thus, in a situation such as use or abuse, it is entirely acceptable to request that a contract be nullified.

If you believe you are in an unhealthy or abusive situation or that you are far away from your life purpose, give your contract to God and ask him to determine whether or not it needs to be revoked. This does not apply to every difficult situation you come across in life. As mentioned before, the lessons you learn in each lifetime as a result of spiritual contracts are important for your soul's development.

Often you will not know what your spiritual contracts involve; thus, it is best to leave them intact, if possible. After completing the Soul Contract Prayer in Chapter 6, if you are still uncertain whether or not to maintain a specific contract you believe is now detrimental to your spiritual growth, place your concern once more in God's hands and be willing to listen for the answer.

Releasing Contracts Prayer

Dear God,

  I am concerned that my contract regarding _____ is keeping me from my life purpose or no longer serves my highest good. If it is Your will, I ask that this contract be removed and released from me in Angelic peace.

~Amen

***

  After completing this prayer, you may receive sudden insight or a feeling about whether or not the contract you inquired about should be released or whether or not you need to ask for other contracts to be broken. We cannot stress enough that releasing contracts and vows for this lifetime, as for all lifetimes, is a choice that should not be taken lightly.

  In releasing agreements for this lifetime, you may find that you are led out of situations that are unhealthy or abusive in nature. It is even possible that your soul began distancing you from these abusive relationships and unhealthy situations from the first moment you read the Life Purpose Prayer at the beginning of this book.

  However, if you are still uncertain as to whether or not a contract should be released, you may need to review your agreements and hear the confessions of your soul. It is important to consider how your soul truly feels about the people, places, situations, and things in your life. A conscious review of each spiritual contract will help you understand whether or not it serves your highest good and should remain a part of your soul's journey. Archangel Michael will help you identify what no longer serves you and will assist in the release of all agreements from this lifetime that are not in your highest good and are no longer in alignment with your life purpose. You may wish to record the following meditation, have someone read it to you, or listen to the pre-recorded meditation available online.

Meditation: Soul Confessions with
Archangel Michael

Find a place where you will not be disturbed, and take a few minutes to go within. Quiet your mind and allow yourself to relax. Take a few deep breaths as you shift yourself into a comfortable position. Allow yourself to drift deeper and deeper into total relaxation. Close your eyes and imagine a blank screen before you. Hold that image as you continue to relax. Any outside noises only serve to deepen your state of relaxation.

Continue taking slow, steady breaths and imagine a slide show of your life projecting on the screen behind your closed eyes. The images of your life slowly shift across the screen, one by one, highlighting the parts of your life you believe to be important. As each image comes into frame, consider the ways in which you believe the person, place, situation, or thing is in alignment with your life purpose. You may ask questions such as, "Am I really attached to that car?" "Is this a good relationship for me?" "Do I truly want this job?"

One by one, allow these images to present themselves to you. When the screen goes dark again, restart the slide projector and allow the images to fill the screen again, one by one. This time, allow your soul to come forward and express how you truly feel about each person, place, situation, or thing. Ask your soul, "Is this in alignment with my highest good?" You may need to remind yourself that an important part of rediscovering your life purpose is the ability to accept these soul confessions.

After careful review of your life, you notice a brilliant blue light on the screen before you. As the light grows larger and larger, you feel warmth and love as it completely fills the screen. Now, watch as Archangel Michael emerges from this light. You realize he has come to assist you in clearing all vows, contracts, and agreements from this lifetime that limit you, are no longer in alignment with your true purpose, or those that no longer serve your highest good.

Say to him, "Archangel Michael, I ask to release all vows, contracts, and agreements that I have taken in this lifetime by my own will that no longer serve my highest good. I ask to release all vows, contracts and agreements that were forced upon me in this lifetime as a result of beliefs structured in lack or limitation, originating in religious doctrine, or involving control. I ask that these vows, contracts, and agreements be revoked now, and that I receive clear understanding of all signs and messages guiding me in the steps necessary to remove these limitations from my life."

Thank Archangel Michael for his assistance and watch as he steps back into the brilliant blue light on the screen. Slowly, the light fades and your screen is once again an empty canvas. Take a moment to reflect upon all that you have accomplished in this meditation. When you are ready, slowly open your eyes, feeling refreshed and ready to continue your spiritual journey.

***

Spiritual contracts can be arranged in a way that you can fulfill in this life regardless of their connections. Take the case of Natalie, to whom the idea of spiritual contracts made perfect sense. In reviewing her life purpose and working through this spiritual process, she found great comfort in knowing that an iron clad agreement for her to marry and have children had been entered into prior to this incarnation. For as long as Natalie could remember, she had always wanted to marry and have a family. Natalie also knew that she had an agreement to have a child with someone but it that was not in her spiritual contract to marry this

91

individual. Although this may seem odd to some, it is an occurrence that has become more and more common over the years.

As you are likely aware, sometimes people are brought into our lives for a specific purpose. Sometimes that purpose is to fulfill a contract we agreed to prior to coming into this lifetime. For Natalie, she understood that she and the father of her child were bound to one another to bear this child and were meant to work together to raise the child. That was the specific contract their souls had agreed upon. To this day, they are each honoring that contract, but separately. Although it took some time, Natalie understands now that this agreement was entered into for her spiritual growth.

Often, these contracts affect souls other than just your own. Natalie recognized that her contract affected her life, as well as the lives of her child and extended family. In addition, she realized that this contract will influence all of the lives her child will impact because of his upbringing and the two parents he chose for himself. While it was unclear to Natalie why she would have made this agreement, she trusted that her soul knew more at that time the contract was conceived than she knows in this lifetime and that this contract was carried through in her highest and best good.

Like Natalie you will notice that some relationships begin to deteriorate over time. As these relationships crumble, there will be little left of them as you step aside and look at the rubble left behind. At first, you may not realize the actions taking place that lead up to the severing of ties. You may notice a shift in your relationships but cannot immediately identify the reason, although you may become aware of some understanding of the dissolution of such relationships over time. It may be difficult to grasp the end of these relationships, but as you have likely observed throughout your lifetime, some relationships are better left undone.

Do not feel that you are meant to remain in an abusive or hostile relationship or that you have done something to deserve this type of treatment. No one deserves hostility or aggression, but it is up to you to stand in your power and say, "Enough is enough." You are worthy of all of the blessings this life has to offer. This includes living your life purpose and recognizing your importance in this world.

Having supportive people by your side during your journey through this lifetime is not over reaching or just wishful thinking. Choose your friends carefully but understand that they may come and go quickly, depending upon how they align with your purpose and the reason for which they were brought into your life in the first place. It is likely you will notice relationships changing faster than ever before, and this distinction is normal and in perfect alignment with your highest good.

Just as you do not deserve to be in a tumultuous relationship; neither do you deserve to be a slave to others. Some people feel that their life purpose is to serve, please, or be kind to everyone around them despite the circumstance. While it is true everyone can use a little more kindness in their lives, your life purpose does not include your servitude to others. Additionally, you likely will not be able to positively affect every single person with whom you come into contact during your life, thus making it difficult to please everyone.

Once you recognize this, you will see how adverse it can be for you to give away your rights to another person. It does not benefit that person the way you intend nor does it benefit you. Because of this, it is important to understand how to set boundaries with other people. Retaining your own power and maintaining positive boundaries is the best way to help someone else because not only are you here in this lifetime to learn, so too are you here to teach. How can another person learn a lesson from you when you are too busy giving them the answers to the challenge? Stop serving them, enabling them, or pandering to them...allow others to learn their own life lessons.

Consider the story of Denise. She went back to a failed relationship with a man she knew was not appropriate for her. The man had been unfaithful to Denise repeatedly yet she continued to return to the relationship again and again. After participating in a past life reading, Denise realized that this man, whom she trusted time and again, was indeed her brother in a previous life. In that past life, he was also an alcoholic whom she felt compelled to help, to her own detriment. She learned that in that past life, Denise gave her brother everything she had; money, time, and love to support him in the best way she could.

Although she believed this was the right thing to do, Denise's efforts in that lifetime were in vain. Her brother did not learn the lessons he was meant to learn because she continued to rescue him and enable him instead of allow him to learn the lessons he arranged to learn in that lifetime: stand on his own two feet, get his life together, and correct his own mistakes. Unfortunately, Denise had enabled her brother to the point where he was unable to accomplish his goal in that lifetime and move forward with his own spiritual growth.

As a result of Denise's failed attempt to teach him this life lesson, and her brother's failed attempt to stand on his own two feet, the lesson was again carried over into the present lifetime and in the context of a different relationship, that of significant others. Thus, in the present lifetime this man had no respect for Denise because she was unable to set healthy boundaries with him. When Denise finally accepts that this man is in her life so that she can teach him this lesson, she will begin to set necessary boundaries, thus encouraging him to truly learn his own life lesson rather than rescuing him as she did in the past. Only then will the possibly exist for them to become allies in future incarnations.

Remember, before you came into this lifetime, you made agreements to teach lessons to others, as well as learn lessons from them, so it is important to keep up your end of the bargain unless you have severed ties with a particular soul. As a teacher in this lifetime, you are not meant to people-please, enable, or be a servant. Instead, you are meant to learn the lessons you designated for yourself and adhere to the contracts you created with others between lifetimes.

As mentioned briefly before, an important aspect of upholding these agreements includes setting boundaries with others, standing in your own power, and releasing all negative relationships. Doing so is not synonymous with lack of love, however. Setting boundaries, asserting your power, and releasing everything of detriment to your life purpose are all representative of the ultimate expression of love…the willingness to be your authentic self.

If you find that you are unable to live as your true self and continue to struggle with boundaries, power, and abusive or unhealthy relationships, it is important to be patient with yourself. The activities within this book represent a process of awareness, assimilation, and adjustment over time. You may wish to return to the Soul Confessions with Archangel Michael Meditation to determine whether your contracts are in alignment with your highest good and do further work with Archangel Michael to release those that are not. Or, you may find that you progress through these exercises with little difficulty. However you approach this material is perfectly acceptable to your unique experience.

Affirmations

For the next three days, we ask that you affirm the following:

I clearly see all signs and messages from the angels directing me on my life path.

I release all spiritual contracts that are abusive or unhealthy and are no longer in alignment with my life purpose.

I release all agreements forced upon me based on beliefs of lack or control or limiting religious doctrine that no longer serve my highest good.

Homework

In your journal, record any contracts you identified during this chapter that need to be dissolved. Record your feelings about this new insight. Then, take a single sheet of paper and write down anyone you noted in your journal who needs to be released from you in this lifetime. Over an open flame, burn the sheet of paper in a symbolic gesture of releasing that which no longer serves you. Imagine the smoke carrying the remnants of that contract to the light to be transmuted into positive energy that may be useful in some way to the world.

Note: Some believe release of anything that no longer serves you is best conducted during the waning moon or a lunar eclipse, although this is not necessary to obtain optimum effect. Your intention is the key to effective release.

Chapter 9

I Trust My Divine Self

As you progress through this book, reciting the prayers and listening to the meditations herein, you will find that it becomes easier to accept movement in the direction of your life purpose. You are destined to fulfill an important mission in this world. As you continue to follow your internal guidance, you will begin to notice that your life path becomes clearer.

During this process, it is important to connect with your true self, your Divine self. Learning to truly trust the Divine self is crucial to your spiritual development. You may initially find trust to be a foreign concept; however, it is an activity you engage in on a daily basis. You trust your vehicle to get you safely from one place to another. You trust the food you eat to nourish your body. You trust your employer to pay you for the work you perform. You trust your intuition to keep you out of dangerous situations. It is this intuition that is linked to your Divine self. Thus, it is this intuition we strive to help you develop in this chapter.

Some call intuition a gut feeling or a knowing. Others explain it as having a sense about something or someone. It is important for you to build trust in your intuition, the feelings of your Divine self. As you practice this skill, try not to over-analyze the process. Know with your soul that you are being led along this journey. Over time, your feelings will become an internal sign guiding you along your life purpose journey. And, at times of uncertainty, your intuition may remind you of or guide you through your next step.

Although it may not seem clear to your natural mind, or the ego, in Spirit you know your life purpose fully and completely at this time. Retrieving this knowledge is simply a matter of trusting in your soul and enlightening your mind. As discussed in previous chapters, you had a hand in creating your life purpose before you ever incarnated into this lifetime; thus, you already understand your purpose on a soul level. As you learn to trust in your Divine self, you will find it easier to access this soul level knowledge and place yourself upon the path best suited to your life purpose.

Interestingly, there are several different paths you may take in living your life purpose. For some, you may need to journey along your path for awhile before you recognize that which your soul already knows. Karen experienced this first hand growing up in a home grounded in the Baptist religious faith. Among other things, Karen was raised to believe these three concepts: one cannot communicate with spirits or angels; guardian angels are only here to watch over and protect, and are not here for guidance; and praying to God is the only means to have your prayers, wishes, or needs answered. Indeed, during those formative years, Karen did not even know spirits or channeling existed, not to mention that she was able to channel Heavenly communication herself.

Karen was not open to the idea of channeling until she reached her late 20s and did not know how to channel until her mid 30s. While her soul knew her life purpose all along, Karen's ego did not accept this until later in her journey. When she finally opened up to channeling, the spiritual side of life suddenly made sense.

Unlike Karen's experience, for some, life purpose may not become evident until the end of life when a review confirms that indeed the purpose has been fulfilled. Although most people would like to know whether or not they achieved their life purpose before they become "too old" to enjoy it, sometimes this is not the case. For those who do not discover their path early on, there may be some lingering uncertainty until the life review, but this is not necessary.

Perhaps you are on this planet to learn the art of self-love in many different ways but do not connect this lesson to the purpose of your soul's journey through this lifetime. If this is your lesson and purpose in this life, you may spend the entire lifetime learning and practicing these skills and not realize you have mastered your mission until you cross over. As you conduct your life review in the afterlife, you will likely find that indeed you mastered your purpose: to love thyself.

It is also possible that you may not see the purpose within yourself, but others will see it clearly. Perhaps your purpose is to incarnate now to enjoy a beautiful family life. Or maybe you are meant to help others through giving the gift of love. You might simply be meant to nurture and provide for others. While these examples may not appear to be life purpose related, even the smallest lesson or gift you may give can be related to your purpose in this life.

Interestingly, you may find that people look up to you and are aware of your worth even if you do not realize it yourself. Over the past couple of years, Karen has been surprised at the number of people who tell her how impressed they are that she is accomplishing her life purpose. While she has not always recognized her own life purpose, others have seen the mission within her because they are open to the signs.

Consider the following scenario: You meet a kind lady at the park one day while walking a friend's dog. She notices that you are struggling to keep the big dog under control and approaches you. She calmly gives the dog a cue then gently explains to you what has transpired between her cue and the improvement in the dog's behavior. You ask a few general questions then ask if she trains dogs for a living. She replies, "Good gracious, no. I don't know enough for that." You can clearly see the true essence of this lady, her purpose in life. She is a natural spirit teacher meant to work with animals, train them, and teach their human companions how to best interact with their furry friends.

You may wonder why the lady fails to see this ability in herself. Unfortunately, she is unaware of her true purpose despite however obvious it may be to other people with whom she interacts in daily life. If this is the path you are traveling, you may be able to resolve the disconnect between what others see in you and what you see in yourself by paying attention to the signs and messages other people give to you.

For those of you who know your purpose clearly and follow your life plan, step-by-step, depending upon the agreements you made prior to incarnating in this lifetime, the journey may seem easier. Consider the case of Emily, born into a prominent musical family. From a very young age, Emily begins music lessons and is drawn to anything musical. She is passionate about everything in life and grows up to love and adore life and sees music in everything she encounters.

Because of this, Emily is able to serve her purpose in a highly influential way because she was gifted with the knowledge of her life purpose as a child. Before she was born, Emily explored her life purpose with the souls who would become her parents in this lifetime. During this time, they developed a plan for their life together and activated it immediately upon Emily's birth.

To some, it may seem as if Emily or her parents had no choice in fulfilling her life plan, but remember, every decision you have to make is a choice. For Emily, she knows whichever choice she makes will take her towards music and helping or healing others through her musical gifts. In each of these choices there are many blessings and opportunities. Like Emily, to know and understand your life purpose, and indeed begin serving that purpose the moment you incarnate, is an chance to explore the many opportunities in life that are closely related to your life purpose.

When Emily grows up, she may find herself teaching at a local school. Perhaps she will become a classical concert pianist or maybe she will own a music store specializing in instruments of antiquity. There are many options Emily can explore to fulfill her life purpose of sharing music with the world, but again, it will all rely upon the decisions she makes throughout her life. Thus, while incarnating into this life knowing the steps that need to be taken to achieve your purpose, the actions you choose to embark upon will determine your course and ultimate path along your journey.

Life lessons often take a long time to learn and fully integrate into your Spirit in order to move to the next level of soul growth. For many, you will not know your life purpose unless you visit with a mystic who possesses a background in uncovering these issues. For others, you may instantly know your life purpose. For some, you will figure out your purpose somewhere along your life path. And for a few, you may have never realized there was really a purpose in life before being introduced to the topic recently or being guided to this book.

Regardless of the path you take, in truth you are the only one who knows your soul and can uncover the mysteries of your true purpose. It is a matter of releasing the ego so that you may see the true you and the path you are meant to travel. As you release the influence of the ego and rediscover your true purpose, you will learn life lessons and overcome obstacles at a more rapid pace. You will find that this enhanced level of learning even occurs within basic situations in life. For example, have you ever wandered off your path or become distracted by insignificant details in some daily task?

Perhaps in going to the refrigerator to get a drink, you set your book down on the counter. You notice something sticky on the counter so you go to the sink to dampen a towel. While at the sink, you realize your plant needs water so you set down the towel and instead water the plant. Then you decide the plant needs more sunlight so you take it outside. While you are outside, you decide to get the mail. It had rained heavily the previous day, so on the way to the mailbox, your foot sinks into the ground. Your shoe is covered in mud so you go to the door, remove your shoe then go inside and sit down on the couch. As you sit there, it finally dawns on you that you do not have your drink, your book, or the mail.

As you can see, the simple journey of getting a drink became complicated by many diversions along the way. Sometimes, staying on our life path is very similar, as distractions and challenges redirect our route. Truly trusting in your intuition and Divine self and recognizing the purpose you are meant to live in this lifetime can help minimize these distractions. Then, instead of walking around the mountain several times to reach your destination, you will go straight to the top and achieve your soul's desires. Indeed, instead of traipsing back and forth in a circuitous path, following the more direct path will help you complete your purpose in a timeframe that serves your highest good.

For those who have recurring and long-standing issues with distraction and have spent hours wondering how to correct this issue, you will easily find a solution as you begin to trust your Divine self. For those who set out looking for something or planning to do a specific task and then get sidetracked by something else, you will improve your ability to focus on what you truly desire and the steps you must take to fulfill your mission. Indeed, in beginning to trust in your Divine self, your intuition, you first need to consider how important it is for you to follow your life purpose. How serious are you about making the changes that will transform your mundane, everyday life into your unique life purpose?

Since you are reading this book, it is likely your answer is a resounding "I'm extremely serious!" With that in mind, you can train yourself to evaluate every aspect of your life to determine if it is in alignment with your purpose, or instead if it is a manifestation of your ego's desires. Do not be afraid to ask yourself, "Is this part of my life purpose or is this a desire born of the ego?" If you remain uncertain, you may wish to further clarify your question. "Am I passionate about this?" It is possible that interests and ideas fall into both categories: life purpose and ego desire. More than likely, however, if you are passionate about something then it is part of your life purpose.

Perhaps you are passionate about working with children but do not want to take the requisite course for a teaching degree.

You may have a way with elderly people but have no interest in working within a skilled nursing facility. Maybe you have always wanted to be a healer but do not agree with the medical field as defined by the western world. Perhaps you love to build and create but find yourself in a clerical position doing the same task every day. While you may not want to take part in the education and experiences your ego believes is required to fulfill any of these interests, if you are passionate about something then it may be a clue about your life purpose. You may need to open your mind and explore non-traditional possibilities to find the answer.

While it is important to learn to trust in your Divine self and increase your intuition, it is often helpful to seek guidance from the Light, especially if you feel you are at a crossroads or do not understand the signs you are receiving. There are many forms of communication you may use with Spirit. Depending upon your own style of communication, you may ask Spirit to answer you with the visual representation of a green light or red light. Some may prefer the auditory expression of 'Yes' or 'No'. Or, you may prefer something completely unique and specific to you. Whichever method you choose, know that in trusting your intuition and practicing your own style of communication with the Light, it will become easier to hear their guidance over time.

In trusting in your Angelic guidance, remember to trust in the drive and desire you express about projects and ideas, as well.

Remember, things that you are passionate about usually lie within both categories: life purpose and ego desire. Do not allow yourself to get swept away by your passions. Be mindful to ask for the truth in each situation, and realize that when you continuously do this you will instinctively begin to ask whether or not something is part of your purpose.

If you feel you are struggling with differentiating between purpose and ego, you are free to ask the following for each concern: "Am I following my purpose by doing this? Am I following my purpose by making this decision or choice? Does this option leave me farther from my truth and my purpose?"

Again, over time you will learn to trust your intuition, your gut feeling, that knowing you receive when you ask a question. Continue to trust your instincts and allow them to develop. But know also that sometimes there are strong lessons that need to be learned in this life. Sometimes you may be taken down roads you never intended to travel. While it may seem disconcerting, any lesson learned is for your highest good. Challenges are part of life.

You will not always travel the perfect road simply because it is part of your path to learn lessons and overcome challenges. However, the universe conspires to give you just those experiences that you chose to have on this planet. Accepting these situations will enable you to complete the highest and best soul growth possible and allow you to confidently move to the next level of growth on your soul's journey.

Remember, every soul on this planet is here to evolve and grow and to help others to evolve and grow, as well. Every soul has their own lessons to learn and also those they must teach to others. This is the reason you made a life purpose plan before you incarnated here on earth. Some souls created a simple plan such as having kids and raising a family. Others have a mission to heal, teach, or write books. And many have a complicated life mission involving any number of smaller purposes to evolve into some significant act that has broader implications for the world. No matter what your mission or life purpose plan, your soul participated in the planning stage and ultimately agreed to each and every aspect involved.

It is important to understand that the planning stage was not necessarily easy. You decided on lessons you wanted to learn and chose other souls to help you learn these lessons. Likewise, you chose others to help guide you along your journey. You may have met with a group of souls who determined what would be the highest potential possible in order for you to accomplish all of the goals and lessons that you would need to both learn and teach in this lifetime.

At some point along your journey, you may have acquired spirit guides who were once family members in this lifetime. While having the guidance of a deceased loved one may seem comforting or positive, their presence in your life may disrupt the plans you previously created. Remember, each soul has its own lessons to learn. Your ancestors have not necessarily evolved to a higher level than you or learned all of the lessons required in the lifetime they recently departed. With that being the case, it is possible they carried baggage with them into the afterlife. When they assume the role of your spirit guide, sometimes this baggage is transferred to you in unsuspecting ways.

Before Karen came out of the "spiritual closet", she was indecisive about what to do with her blossoming spiritual connection. She constantly worried about what other people would think or say about her, and dwelled on whether she would be accepted by others. Despite this, she continued to feel drawn towards interacting with the Angels and strengthening her abilities.

In 2012, Karen decided to seek guidance about her dilemma from the Angels who had been helping her hone her abilities. Despite the Angels' insistence that she was ready, Karen continued to hide her spiritual worth, gifts, and interests. She knew she was hearing their guidance correctly and that her channeling abilities had greatly improved over time, yet Karen's debilitating fear prevented her from revealing her true self.

Karen continued to explore the reason she felt so conflicted. The Angels soon revealed that her great grandmother, Helen, who passed away many decades before, was one of her guides in

Spirit. From beyond, Grandmother Helen perpetuated a narrative that became the foundation for Karen's fears. "People will make fun of you. They will no longer like or appreciate you if you tell them what you can do with your gifts." Subconsciously, Karen heard these messages, accepted them, and believed them to be truth.

Knowing this information, Karen was able to make a more informed choice about her own spiritual development. She asked the Angels to remove her great grandmother as one of her guides in Spirit so that she would no longer be influenced by the narrative of fear. Almost immediately after the Angels removed Grandmother Helen from Karen's spiritual council, Karen noticed that her mood lighten and she felt a sense of complete peace. Within days she created a social media account to share her gifts and new found confidence with the world.

The fear of acceptance that Karen experienced was based on the insecurities of someone else…her great grandmother. Unbeknownst to her at the time, Karen had falsely accepted those thoughts, desires, and opinions based in fear as her own. Although her grandmother had good intentions and Karen was grateful for her counsel, with the Angels' assistance, she realized it did not serve her highest good to have Grandmother Helen as a guide in this lifetime.

While some erroneously believe that when a loved one crosses over they suddenly have all of the answers to life, this is not always the case. As mentioned previously, your loved ones who have passed do not necessarily possess a greater knowledge than you and sometimes carry their own baggage with them into the afterlife. Not only do their personalities and opinions remain intact, your loved ones on the other side of the veil continue to learn and grow spiritually until they decide to reincarnate into a new life on the Earthly plane. Thus, it is critical to develop your intuition and learn to trust your instincts so that you may release any guides who are not in alignment with your highest good.

Like Karen, you may find yourself moving away from the company of those who seek the guidance of deceased loved ones. Instead of allowing the opinions of your Earthly ancestors to influence or guide you through this process of rediscovering your life purpose, you will come to rely on only beings of the highest light.

Similarly, there may be spirits who are not your ancestors but who have attached themselves to you as negative energy anyway. It is possible that you remind them of someone else or perhaps they are simply mischievous. These spirits can deplete your energy and cause havoc in your life. Trust in your Divine self to help you determine if one of these energy hijackers has infiltrated your energy field. If you suspect that unwelcome spirit energy has attached to you, return to Chapter 5 and complete the Cord Cutting with Archangel Michael Meditation. This will assist in clearing away all negative energies and entities that do not serve your highest good.

After severing all cords with unwelcome energies or spirits who do not serve your highest good, begin a new pattern in your life. From this point forward, ask that your guides be for your highest good and of the highest light so that you may confidently move ahead with your life purpose. Karen is certain that if she had continued to follow her deceased great grandmother's guidance, she would not have moved forward with her purpose in this lifetime.

Some people spend their entire life searching for their life purpose only to find it was staring them in the face the entire time. Why couldn't they see it? Why didn't they know? How could it be so simple? Your life purpose does not need to be complex or significant to others. It is a contract you created before coming into this lifetime and it bears your soul's fingerprint. Your contract contains all of the experiences you want to have in this lifetime to advance your spiritual growth. Perhaps you experienced many difficult lives on this Earth and decided that you simply wanted to enjoy the state of 'being' this time around.

Dr. Gale found herself pondering this very question about her young son. He was such a fun loving boy and enjoyed people, animals, adventures, everything, but above all, he loved playing. Dr. Gale frequently wondered what he might like to do

114

for a profession when he was older. She hoped to find activities that matched his desires so that she may guide him as best she could. Whenever Dr. Gale asked her son what he would like to do when he grew up, he would answer very simply, "Be a kid." Dr. Gale pondered this comment for years.

During a chance encounter at a Mind-Body-Spirit event in Pennsylvania in 2013, Dr. Gale was guided to a spiritual intuitive and teacher who was conducting readings at the event. The spiritual intuitive explained that Dr. Gale's son was an old soul and had learned many lessons throughout his lifetimes. He had worked hard and was ready to enjoy this lifetime. His soul's contract for this lifetime was simply to relax, have fun, and play.

Like Dr. Gale's son, some people's life purpose is as easy as enjoying their life. It may seem simplistic, but it is an important life purpose nonetheless. Every soul has a different goal in this lifetime and some people are meant to just 'Be'. If this is your purpose in this lifetime and you endlessly search for some big mission in life, you will never find it. Failing to see the glory of your purpose will leave you feeling disillusioned even though you are already living your life purpose by simply existing. Trust in your Divine guidance to help you determine whether or not this is a possibility for you and to guide you down the best path for fulfilling your mission.

No matter which path you are traveling or what purpose your soul strives to achieve in this lifetime, you will find that it is

115

important to reflect upon those things your soul desired for you to learn and experience along your journey of spiritual growth. In fulfilling your life purpose you will find that you no longer need to incarnate over and over to repeat the same lesson. You will see that learning your lessons the first time around is truly the best way. Continue using your own unique method of communicating with your guides and Angels as a beneficial technique for recording your process of transformation and realignment with your life purpose. With practice, you will find that the process of aligning with your authentic self and fulfilling your purpose becomes easier both in this lifetime and through the ages.

Affirmations

For the next three days, we ask that you affirm the following:

Joy fills me when I am on my true path.

I remove from me anything that does not serve my highest good now and forever.

I accept my Divine truth.

I easily recognize my true path and purpose.

I gracefully accept my Divine self.

I trust in my Divine guidance.

Homework

Take a few moments to reflect on your thoughts and feelings about your Divine truth. Conduct an interview with your true self in a candid and open manner. As you record your responses, do not allow the ego to interfere. Use this assignment as a training tool to help you express and receive your true feelings rather than those of the ego. The following are a list of possible interview questions:

Am I currently on my life path?

What steps do I need to take to be on my life path?

What is the foundation for my life purpose?

In what situations can I express my life purpose?

What aspects of the ego are holding me back from living my Divine truth?

How can I overcome the hurdles of my ego so that I may live my life purpose?

Chapter 10

I Forgive Myself and Others

Society, in a general sense, has learned over time that holding on to negative feelings regarding a person or situation can create anger and resentment which may ultimately lead to stress, anxiety, and/or depression in our lives. For some, this may cause stagnation or an inability to find the path we should take in life. For others, these negative feelings manifest as health or relationship problems. While most of us were taught the importance of forgiveness from a very early age, over time, the pressures of daily life and compounding frustrations have contributed to us forgetting this important and life-affirming process.

Whether you first learned about forgiveness from religious parable related to you as a child, as stories passed down from family members through the generations, from the counselor you saw many years ago, or from experience, the act of forgiveness, or lack thereof, continues to play a significant role in your life. Forgiveness is not an act of forgetting what has transpired but rather, an act of releasing negativity and unhealthy connections to people who have cause us harm in some way. And while we tend to think of forgiveness as a peace offering we bestow upon someone else, often the person we most need to forgive is the self...you.

Unforgiveness is a burden. We carry it across our shoulders like the proverbial albatross in the old story about the sailor and the whale. It is only when we capture or defeat the subject of our anger that we feel truly relieved...but do we really? Likely, the task of carrying that burden, that anger has caused other problems in our lives. In some way, chasing after that whale all these years later, we missed the beauty and joy in life. Rather, we were too busy struggling with unforgiveness to fully experience and enjoy life.

For some, this struggle of being unable to forgive ourselves or others may have held us back from our life purpose. Instead, we cling to bitterness and an unwillingness or inability to move

120

forward in life. This stagnant energy consistently interferes with your thoughts, feelings, and actions as you continue to dwell upon the past and all of its related tragedies and dramas. By holding onto this negative energy, you are relegated to relive the experience over and over again which serves to keep you in a holding pattern where you experience very little soul growth. It is almost as if your soul is frozen in time and unable to remove itself from the past. One of the questions Dr. Gale and Karen are each frequently asked is "How do I learn to forgive?"

One of the most important aspects of forgiveness involves one key component…you. In learning forgiveness, it is crucial to begin with self-forgiveness. Sometimes this may involve repeated practice. But remember, any attempt at self-forgiveness is successful. For in the recognition of the need to forgive and in the act of trying to forgive the self, your intention to forgive helps you achieve your goal.

When you begin the process of self-forgiveness, you will need to do so for everything you thought you should have done and everything you regret doing. In many ways, the should haves, could haves, and would haves can prove quite debilitating. As you may have learned, second guessing yourself only serves to increase the burden you carry. Remember, every choice you make in life brings you an opportunity for a life lesson. And because you are in the perpetual process of learning, second guessing the choices you have made serves no purpose other than weighing you down emotionally and spiritually.

The question becomes, "Why would you want to further burden yourself?" The response we hear most often is simple but tragic: "I deserve it." In other words, "I deserve this burden. I deserve this self doubt. I deserve what I get." But truly, there is nothing you could ever do that cannot be forgiven. You deserve forgiveness.

Forgiveness of self is an important component to progressing along your life path. The following request is intended to help you align with your life path at this present moment. From time to time along your journey, you may need to revisit this request if you believe you have additional unforgiveness to release. When you are ready, find a quiet place where you can have a few moments to yourself. Take a few deep breaths, close your eyes, and relax so that it will be easier to go within your heart. When you are relaxed, open your eyes and state the following request in your mind or aloud.

Spiritual Request: Self-Forgiveness

Dear Archangel Raphael,

I reach out to you now with love and humility in my heart. Please help me forgive myself for any and all situations in my past where I have held onto guilt, shame, hostility, and/or pride. Please open my heart and show me how to release the past and bring forgiveness to myself. I ask that you lift this burden from me now. As the weight is removed from my soul, I release to the light all pain, suffering, and abuse so that it may be transmuted into love.

From this point forward, I take with me only the lessons and benefits necessary for my soul's growth. Help me recognize that I am a sacred member of the human race and that I am also Spirit with a soul residing within this body. I ask for healing of every part of this body and soul. Please ease the painful memories from my mind that result in unforgiveness of self. I ask that this pain no longer weighs upon my heart, body or mind in any capacity.

From this point forward, I release all toxins and stale energies that I have held in my body through fear and grief and all energies or entities that remind me of these grievances as they are no longer needed in my memory bank. Please help me master the art of trusting myself and living in Angelic Peace.

Thank you for your healing, Archangel Raphael, and for helping me to learn to forgive myself and release past hurt.

***

Releasing and forgiving are two powerful tools. In previous chapters, we have discussed the importance of releasing all that no longer serves us. As you have learned, one aspect of moving along your life path or simply moving forward into the future involves releasing the baggage of the past that has only served to weigh you down. When you add forgiveness to your spiritual toolbox, the benefits of these two powerful techniques combine to free you from unnecessary burden so that you may complete your life mission.

Many of us have carried this baggage of past hurts or unforgiveness for so long that it has become a normal part of life. You may feel naked or incomplete without the chaos of the past constantly resurfacing in your life. You may wonder whether it is even necessary to forgive and release these burdens in order to complete your life purpose. Some may dwell on the possibility that forgiving must mean excusing the hurtful act in some way.

As you begin to release the ties that connect you to the past, you will find that these concerns and others begin to melt away. You will find that you no longer need the reminder, the chaos, or the pain. And when you allow Spirit to help you release these ties, you gain a loving and powerful advocate in your overall pursuit of spiritual development.

Releasing Unforgiveness Prayer

Dear God,

I release to you all stubborn or blocked energy that I have carried within my heart. Where I have held unforgiveness,

124

bitterness, unworthiness, or unhealthy expectations for myself and others, I ask that you remove this energy and transmute it into positive energy that will be a benefit to this world. Knowing that all things are truly taken care of in the spirit of the highest light, I now release all worries. I reject any distress and drama of the past and accept a future free from reproach.

~Amen

***

As you progress along the path of forgiveness, you may wonder how you can discern whether or not the process is working. What signs indicate that healing is taking place? How do I know any of this is working? Your signs will be unique to you but may include an increased ability to let go of troubling situations with ease; a decrease in the number of difficult past situations that you allow into your consciousness; a decrease in the amount of time you spend dwelling on memories of situations that once angered you; a reduction in the negative feelings associated with people who hurt you at some time in the past; or perhaps a feeling of lightness spreading across your body as if heavy weights have been lifted from your soul.

Through this process, you will learn to honor yourself and your ability to let go of what no longer serves you, including any residual unforgiveness that knowingly or unknowingly has lodged in your heart, mind, and soul. For some, the power of releasing and forgiving creates an immediate lifting sensation which in turn promotes a palpable sense of freedom from unseen constraints. For others, the benefits may be observed over a period of time, culminating in a gradual sense of freedom. Periodic review of this chapter may be necessary to strengthen your resolve and create an environment wherein forgiveness becomes habit.

Meditations

The following meditations are designed to assist you in releasing the past and the burden of unforgiveness. You may wish to do them in order, skip around, or choose only those that resonate with you. Whatever choice you make is the perfect choice for you at this very moment in time. You may wish to revisit this section as you journey along your life path to reinforce your new habit of forgiveness and release.

Meditation: Releasing the Weight of Unforgiveness

Each moment of our lives culminates in feelings, emotions, thoughts, and experiences. As we move through our lives in linear fashion, some of these moments become embedded in our memories, our cells, and our hearts for good or bad. While it is always pleasant reliving the memory of these positive moments, it is the negative moments we more frequently recall. And as we do the weights of these memories bear down upon us.

As you rest in a comfortable position now, begin to settle into an inviting space where you will not be disturbed. Allow your mind to travel back in time to a peaceful experience in your life. It may be a tranquil walk through the woods, perhaps a calm evening on the beach listening to the waves lap at the sand, or maybe the quietude and beauty of your baby sound asleep in the nursery. Whatever moment you choose to reflect on is just right for you. Allow this experience to penetrate your being. Feel the peace, comfort, and complete tranquility of the moment.

Remain in this place for a few more minutes and allow a memory of something negative to come into your awareness. Perhaps it was an argument with a loved one, a disagreement between friends, or hurtful expressions from your co-workers. Whatever the memory, allow it now to intrude on your peaceful moment. Feel the weight of it in your shoulders, the burden of unforgiveness in your heart. As we practice the art of forgiveness, it is not necessary to condone any travesty against us, nor do we approve of our own travesty against another. For now, just breathe and notice harm that has been done. Notice the excess weight you have been carrying around.

You may recognize that as humans, we make mistakes and that we all carry varying levels of this weight around with us.

But, these burdens need not consume us or prevent us from enjoying our lives, living in the moment, free from unnecessary hardship and pain. As you continue breathing under this weight, consider how you might feel with this burden removed. Does it make your pleasant memories that much happier? Does it relieve you of tension or worry? Does it allow for the reconciliation of an important relationship? Does it allow forgiveness of self and others?

Remove those weights now and allow forgiveness into your heart. Feel the simplicity and ease with which you can move through life without these weights. In your mind, focus again on the peaceful moment with which you began this meditation. Feel the lightness in your mood, the pressure relieved from your shoulders, the ache removed from your heart. Engage in the moment and feel the expansion of tranquility. Realize how easy it is to forgive yourself and others and to release the burdens that have bound you to a life of unhappiness, distress, and pain.

Take a moment now to call upon Archangel Raphael for healing of these burdens. Allow his healing green light to completely fill you, permeating all aspects of your heart, mind, and body to cleanse and heal you of any negative energy. Imagine these burdens lifting from your body and carrying upward into the heavens to be transmuted into loving energy before raining back down upon the Earth to offer healing to others. Thank Archangel Raphael as he disappears into his peaceful green light.

Returning to the present time you will carry back with you everything that instills peace, love, and forgiveness in your heart and mind. Your memories have been cleansed and your burdens lifted. At the count of three you will rejoin the present moment and feel completely refreshed. One...shifting your body...two...opening your eyes...and three...awake, alert, and ready to go forth with your day.

Meditation: Rewriting the Past for Healing

Let us take a few moments to go back in time, back to a moment when all was not forgiven, a place where wounds were created and began to fester. Find somewhere that you may rest and will not be disturbed for several minutes. Close your eyes as we begin a process of relaxation. Let us first tense our body. Feel your hands clench and your muscles tighten. Now release. Tense your legs and feel how they strain and pull at you. Now release. Tense your neck and shoulders, hold for a moment as you feel the tension building. Now release. Continue this process of tensing and releasing until you believe you have released all stress and strain from your body.

The feeling of releasing this tension is liberating. All of the worries of the day seem to melt away. You are relaxing into a space of peace and comfort. Outside noises only serve to help you go deeper and deeper into this state of relaxation. No worries, no stress, no tension. In this space, you are the creator of your inner world. You are the director of your life. In this relaxed state, you can make anything happen, even the seemingly impossible.

In this tranquil space you can do anything, create anything, or change anything to reflect the desires of your soul and the needs of your heart. You are in the director's chair. What scenes will you reflect upon today? Take a moment to identify a memory from your past where all was not forgiven or hurts were created. In this meditation, you are the director, not the actor. Notice the Angels standing in the background as your production team, waiting to assist you in recreating this masterpiece, this memory from your past.

Watch as the scene materializes before you as if you are on the set of a motion picture. Look carefully at this example of a troubling time in your life. When you are ready, say 'Action' and allow the scene to play out before you. When the scene is over, you may say 'Cut' to end the moment, giving you time to reflect. Observe the scenery. Is it accurate, is everything in place? Is there anything external that contributed to a problem arising in this moment that you should remove from the scene now? If so, remove it.

Now, observe the actors. How are they dressed, are their body movements correct, is there anything you should change about their appearance that could reduce conflict? What about the script? Are the words used between actors filled with anger, frustration, sadness, regret, or fear? If so, change the script now. Use the power of your mind to rewrite this story from your life. What could have been said or done differently? You may wish to ask the Angels if they have any suggestions, as well.

When you are ready, direct the actors to do another 'Take' of the scene, this troubling moment in your life. When you believe everything is ready and the actors know their new lines, say 'Action'. Allow the revisions of your life to play out before you. Notice how the changes to the script allow for forgiveness and healing between all characters. Notice Archangel Raphael step forward and extend his hands towards you. Feel his radiant green healing energy flowing through you now. Feel the peacefulness settle in your heart. Allow Archangel Raphael's healing light to cleanse and clear any last vestiges of hurt or unforgiveness that remain.

As Archangel Raphael returns to your angelic team, thank him for his healing and thank your team for their loving guidance. As you prepare to return to your day, take with you only feelings that will perpetuate a sense of peace, love, comfort, and forgiveness. Allow yourself to gently return to your daily life by slowly shifting your body, stretching, opening your eyes, feeling alert, exhilarated and ready to continue with your day.

Meditation: Mending a Broken Heart

Take some time to get into a comfortable position lying flat on your back, if possible. Focus on your breathing as your body and mind begin to relax. Allow a soft, gentle wave of light to slowly sweep across you, as if tucking you in for an afternoon nap. Feel the warmth of this light spread throughout your tired or sore muscles releasing tension as it spreads. Sink further into the comfort beneath you and imagine that you are on a soft bed of clouds, completely supported in every way.

You may begin to notice the soft beating of your heart as it echoes within your mind. Slow, steady beats…one, two, three…each beat deepens your state of relaxation. Take a moment to look within your heart. For this meditation, become an observer of your heart. What you see within will not affect you in this meditation or beyond. You are simply observing and reporting back to your mind. What do you see? Do you see happiness or sorrow?

You may see happiness with moments of sorrow. Or, you may see only sorrow as the heart seems broken beyond repair. Continue to breathe slowly and deeply as you observe the heart. You may feel that mending a broken heart is elusive or too difficult. In truth, a heart does not really break. The sorrow you have experienced is an illusion created by your mind. It is true that it may take a few months to heal the wounds inflicted upon the heart, but these wounds can indeed be healed. Repeated practice with this meditation can help restructure your thoughts and generate healing from within for both your mind and your heart.

Imagine for a moment that your entire body is encased in a brilliant white light. You are safe, peaceful, and completely relaxed in this state. Watch as your team of angels and guides come to stand beside you, one by one, surrounding you in a circle of love and light, until finally you feel the beautiful loving energy of Archangel Chamuel. Notice that his energy has a soft pinkish glow to it, radiating out and toward you, directly into your heart.

Feel the love of Archangel Chamuel flowing towards you on the current of light. Feel the love of your angels and guides completely enfolding you in this beautiful light. Within this moment of love, ask that all memories that have caused you pain and heartbreak be lifted from you now. As this negative energy releases from you, ask that any energy that is negatively affecting your heart be removed now and forever, in all directions of space and time.

Release this energy now and allow it to float up into the heavens where it may be cleansed and transformed into pure love. Know that this light works as a powerful force to remove and cleanse these energies from your heart. Where the negative emotions, sorrow, and hurt once dwelled within your heart, imagine this space filling with brilliant pink light...every hole, every shard, and every memory.

Now bring the light up to your throat. Imagine the loving pink energy transforming into a cleansing white light. Take a moment to forgive yourself for any times when you did not speak up for yourself in relationships or for when you did not speak your truth with respect to love. You are no longer a victim. You are strong. And you are fearless in love.

Allow this cleansing light to scan you for any residual darkness or negative energies that may be lingering and release. Let go of everything that no longer serves you. Allow the light to fill you completely and heal your heart and your truth. Repeat in your mind...I now allow myself to speak my truth at all times. Feel one last infusion of love from Archangel Chamuel and your team of angels and guides. Watch as they return to be one with the light surrounding you, filling you to completion.

Slowly begin to reconnect with your surroundings, carry this love as you return. Begin to shift your position and move your fingers as you fully reintegrate with your consciousness. Open your eyes and return to your day refreshed, rejuvenated, and completely immersed in love of self and all things in the Universe.

Meditation: Forgiving the Past

Take a few moments to sit or lie back in a comfortable position and begin a process of relaxation. Whatever technique you feel most comfortable using to invite a measure of calm and peace into your body and mind is just perfect for this meditation. You may choose to take deep relaxing breaths. You may choose to slowly count your breaths. You may choose to tense and relax each part of your body, beginning at your feet and moving up to the top of your head, or the reverse, starting at your head and moving down to your feet.

You may choose a visualization technique that takes you further and further into your mind. Or, you may use guided imagery as you walk through that special peaceful space in your heart. Whichever technique you use is just right for you in this moment. Allow the sound of my voice to take you deeper and deeper into a peaceful state.

Notice the tension and worry leaving your body, slipping away like water flowing down a drain. Notice your thoughts coming and going. It is not necessary to give them any attention at this time, simply allow yourself to observe them then watch them pass by. Allow any negativity that may have attached itself to you to flow down this drain, as well, as you continue relaxing deeper and deeper with the sound of my voice.

135

You may begin to notice that your body feels very heavy, very relaxed, and very peaceful as the stresses of the day float away. Allow this moment of tranquility to expand throughout your body and deep into your mind. As the peacefulness envelopes you, notice a blank screen projected before your mind's eye. Perhaps the screen is surrounded by a beautiful golden frame. Or, perhaps it is a white screen offset by rich, crimson curtains in the fashion of an old movie theatre. Or, maybe this screen presents to you as a simple blank slate. It is not important whether this screen is minimal or elegant, large or small...it is only important that you feel a deep sense of relaxation as you gaze upon it.

Now, notice the remote control that operates the screen within your mind. When you are ready, press the play button and allow visions of your past to begin slowly playing across this screen, filling your mind with images of a peaceful moment in your life. Feel this scene taking you even deeper into the peace and tranquility that fills you now. In a moment, I will count to five and ask that you push the button on your remote to take you to a different point in time. As you move through the scenes in your life, you are safe and protected, witnessing the images on a screen rather than in person.

You remain deeply relaxed as you follow the sound of my voice. Five...deep relaxation fills you...four...moving deeper and deeper into your memories...three...safe and protected…two…locating a moment of pain or trauma…and one…you press the button and a troubling memory from your past begins to play across the screen. View the images as if watching a movie. No part of this scene can hurt you. You are safe and protected. Allow this memory to play out before you, but realize that the emotion associated with the memory is fading away. Any negative emotions such as anger, fear, hate, and frustration begin to dissipate. As these negative emotions dissolve, you feel a sense of peace come over you as you begin to forgive the past. You realize that without the emotion, the memory of this once painful time in your past becomes less powerful, less hurtful, and less controlling of your life.

With the release of these emotions and the new found forgiveness for your past, you notice the images on the screen begin to fade. As all remaining vestiges of negativity melt away and the gift of forgiveness fills you completely, the memory before you fades from the screen, forever releasing the control that it once had over your life.

With a shimmering blank screen before you, it is time to realize that you can write your own history in a way that supports and encourages you to move forward in life. Releasing all pain, suffering, and abuse from your past and allowing the gift of forgiveness to take its place cleanses your heart and mind and gives you freedom to begin this day as a brand new life.

In a moment, I will count to five to bring you back to the present time. As you prepare to return, you will bring with you this sense of forgiveness, freedom, contentment, and intention to begin your life anew. One...forgiveness in your heart and mind. Two...the feeling of freedom completely fills you. Three...carrying the intention to have a peaceful, joyful life. Four...returning to the present moment. And five...eyes open, awake, alert, and ready to continue your day.

***

The spoken and written word carries with it extremely powerful intent. Often, it is not sufficient to simply speak words of forgiveness in the mind, but rather to speak them aloud or write a letter explaining our feelings and our intent of forgiveness. These words may be intended for the self or for others; although, it is not necessary that anyone else ever witnesses the words for them to be effective.

Sometimes, this technique is especially helpful when we feel shame or embarrassment for something we have done or when someone has hurt us so egregiously that we do not believe we could ever forgive. Fortunately, there is nothing that cannot be forgiven if you have a willing heart.

It may be helpful to remember that the weight of unforgiveness does not hold anyone else back from their life journey. However, these burdens may result in inhibiting your own spiritual growth. Dr. Gale often recommends the letter writing technique in her clinical practice as a tool to help her patients express their feelings and release any pain that has lingered as a result of unforgiveness or tragedy of some kind. For those not interested in expressing their feelings in writing, you may prefer the spoken word technique. Each process is powerful in its own right, but you should choose whichever technique best suits you.

Letter Writing Technique

This technique involves putting pen to paper. This letter may be addressed to you, someone else, your Angels, or even the Divine. You may choose to use special paper or a treasured pen for this process. The materials you choose are not important unless you want them to be important. While there are many topics you could include in this letter, below are some examples of topics and phrases that may help you get started:

I recognize that it is time to forgive all who have harmed me, upset me, or hurt me in any way throughout my life.

I feel that I cannot forgive _____.

I know the time has come to release _____ from the hurt that he/she caused.

I forgive _____ for the hurt that he/she caused me.

I release all energy associated with the hurt that

_____ caused.

While these are just examples of the many topics you may wish to address, it is by no means exhaustive. For the best result possible, you may wish to include an explanation of what you learned from the person who hurt you, even if the lesson seems negative. For example, you may write, "As a result of my relationship with you and the multiple times you stole from me, I learned to be more careful about whom I trust." Most importantly, you must allow all to be forgiven and to truly forgive those who have hurt you. The act of allowing is powerful and expresses your willingness to move forward.

After you finish writing your letter and are satisfied with the thoughts and feelings you have expressed, in addition to your intention to forgive, you may choose to read your letter aloud, although it is not necessary. When it is time to release your intention to the universe, there are a variety of methods you can use. One of the most frequently used methods of release involves burning the letter which allows its healing message to be carried on the wind. Another method involves submerging your letter in water for a period of time which serves to symbolically wash away the pain and unforgiveness you have been carrying with you. Similarly, you may choose to bury your letter in the ground as if planting a seed so that your intention for forgiveness may give life to new spiritual growth.

For some, the art of forgiveness becomes a process whereby smaller issues are forgiven first then larger issues until finally the greatest issues of all are forgiven through a series of letters over a period of time. For others, the process is relatively brief and may require only one letter. There is no one perfect way to achieve forgiveness as it is greatly dependent upon your own spiritual growth and life path.

Some people prefer to perform this process as part of a ritual while others are not concerned with rituals. Either way is acceptable as long as the intention for forgiveness is pure. Additionally, any method you choose to release the words in your letter is right for you in this moment. Regardless of the variations you decide to use in the letter writing technique, the purpose of this process is to release the energy from your body and send it into the light where it can be transmuted into love and forgiveness.

Spoken Word Technique

For those who are not comfortable with the process of writing or for those who feel their spoken words carry more power, you may prefer to speak your words of forgiveness aloud. Before you begin this process, allow yourself to be in a comfortable state where you will not be disturbed so that you are truly free to verbally express your thoughts and feelings. In constructing your intent, it is important to include the same elements described in the written word technique. Allow your thoughts and feelings to flow from your heart center. If you feel yourself become angry or frustrated as you express yourself, acknowledge those feelings for a moment then take a deep breath and release them. While it is important to identify and acknowledge any feelings that arise during this process, dwelling on negativity or prolonging your distress does not serve you or the benefits of this activity. You may choose to end your oration with a simple statement of forgiveness or you may wish to be more elaborate. A more detailed explanation of forgiveness may include the following:

"I forgive you and release you now. You no longer have control over me. I take back my power from (you/this situation/this time) in my life. I refuse to dwell on this issue any further."

As you complete your statement of forgiveness, close your eyes and imagine a beautiful light surrounding your mind and the words you spoke. As your light-encased words float up into the universe, allow the light to heal the memories from your mind, body, and soul. You may wish to imagine your heart surrounded by a light pink mist to help free you from heartache, or if necessary, heal a broken heart. Similarly, you may wish to envision your throat chakra encased in cleansing blue light as you speak your truth.

***

Because every being experiences stress, trauma, and events in life differently, the timeline for healing and manifestation of the healing benefits of the forgiveness process vary from person to person. No two individuals experience the power of forgiveness in the same way. This is perfectly natural...this is the human experience. Thus, for maximum benefit, it is necessary to be compassionate with yourself. Withhold any judgment of yourself and comparisons with others during this process. You deserve the full benefit of peace in your life and peace in your heart.

For some, the transformation in their lives and their beings will be dramatic and immediate. For others, a more subtle shift in the energy fields will occur. You may find it necessary to repeat these techniques, meditations, and visualizations over a period of days, weeks, or months. Whatever feels right to you is exactly right for you in this moment.

Affirmations

For the next three days, we ask that you affirm the following:

I am confident in my ability to forgive.

I am worthy of forgiveness.

I trust myself to forgive those who have hurt me.

I easily forgive myself and others.

My decisions are my own and I choose forgiveness.

I forgive and am forgiven.

Homework

After completing the forgiveness technique that most resonates with you, take a few moments later in the day to reflect on your experience. From your heart center, assess whether this exercise had immediate results or whether it would be helpful to repeat the forgiveness technique. If you choose to repeat the technique, go within yourself and ask, "When would be the most beneficial time for me to repeat the forgiveness technique?" Listen to your intuition and note in your journal when you will repeat the process.

Final Thoughts

Over the past few centuries, a great shift in awareness has occurred across the globe as people of all walks of life, all dispositions, all cultures, and all nations awaken to the new energies pouring forth into the collective consciousness. Like many of those who came before us, we are expanding our level of spiritual understanding in ways rarely understood by those not yet in sync.

As we continue to synchronize with the universe and allow her knowledge to pour forth, at times we feel misunderstood, ill-informed, uncertain, and lost on our journey. Fortunately, the angels and the Divine are always by our side. When we tune in to the guidance they provide, our way can become less troubled, pieces of the puzzle will likely fall into place, and we will have confidence in self and the situations we experience. Expanding our awareness need not be a traumatic process or a burden, for this awareness is made of light and love.

As you work through these chapters and exercises, it is our greatest wish that you expand your openness to the Divine and your spiritual team. It is with their guidance that you will rediscover your life purpose for this incarnation. In understanding your purpose, you can live your life to the fullest while learning all the lessons you need along the path in full alignment with soul and the love within your heart for everyone and everything you touch.

As mentioned previously, you may need to repeat some of the exercises within this book. Be patient and forgiving with yourself as you do so. Aligning with your truth and your authentic self may take time, and it is during this precious time that you will learn valuable lessons about your Spirit.

You will find that many of the prayers, affirmations and guided meditations may be used throughout your life for various purposes. Consider this a perpetual gift of the Angels. And to further the guidance offered by the Angelic Realm, we invite you to join us for the next installment in this Spiritual Development Series…everything you want to know about affirmations, their power, and their place within your life. Since what you think…you attract, let us help you change your way of thinking to attract everything that will benefit you in this life, everything that is for your highest and greatest good, everything that the Divine has already set aside just for you.

We wish you love, abundance, and great success on this journey through life. Our highest, most loving thoughts are with you as you seek a greater level of enlightenment and allow the Divine into your heart. Go forward on this journey with your hand in ours and the spiritual teams of everyone reading this book by your side. For, truly we are all one, and we are all divine.

Gale Minchew, PhD Over the years, Dr. Gale has been intrigued by paranormal, metaphysical & spiritual concepts. As a child, she had a recurring ethereal experience she could never explain, as well as recurring dreams. Like so many other children, she pushed these experiences aside. She briefly pursued this interest as a teenager. As an adult, she pursued the field of psychology, not realizing it was simply a stepping stone towards her life purpose. Eventually, Dr. Gale graduated with a Doctoral Degree in Counseling Psychology and opened a private practice as a Licensed Psychologist. In 2010, Dr. Gale encountered a renewed interest in the paranormal, metaphysical & spiritual realms. She began studying a broad range of topics, including meditation, regression and hypnotherapy. Between 2011 and 2013, Dr. Gale published four books in the Shadows of Destiny Saga, a series about a young lady with spiritual abilities. It was during this time that Dr. Gale realized she is a spiritual intuitive and her life purpose is that of healer and teacher. It is her goal to help others heal and awaken to their own spiritual abilities. Dr. Gale has published guided meditations on YouTube and has an avid interest in travel to spiritual, metaphysical, and culturally rich locations across the globe.

Karen Lovero Her training to become a channel began in 2004 when Karen was prayed over and received the Holy Spirit. At this time, and with many questions in mind, the gifts of the Holy Spirit were imparted to Karen, prompting a spiritual journey that would lead her down a path she never expected. She soon realized that the church did not understand or accept her spiritual gifts and she would be required to learn about her gifts on her own. As a result, Karen developed a strong connection with the Archangels, Ascended Masters, and God. For the past 10 years, she has trained under the teachings and guidance of the Archangels. As a result of her dedication to this training, Karen is a channel for the Archangels and Masters of the highest light. In addition to her training as a channel, Karen is a Certified Angel Card Reader who studied under Doreen Virtue. She conducts online readings through social media and occasionally presents at workshops near her home in Florida. Her greatest passion is spending time with her children.